Packard

THE WARREN YEARS

By Terry Martin

To Paul
Terry Martin

First Edition
Copyright © 2006 Historical Publishing Network and The National Packard Museum
All rights reserved. No part of this book may be reproduced in any form
or by any means, electronic or mechanical, including photocopying, without
permission in writing from the publisher. All inquiries should be addressed to
Historical Publishing Network, 11555 Galm Road, San Antonio, Texas, 78254.
Phone (210) 688-9006.

ISBN: 978-1-893619-61-6
Library of Congress Card Catalog Number: 2006929689

Packard: The Warren Years

by Terry Martin

PRINTED IN THE UNITED STATES OF AMERICA

This book is dedicated to

the Volunteers of

the National Packard Museum.

Without them it would not be able to function.

James Ward Packard
1863-1928
President and General Manager

George Lewis Weiss
1862-1945
Vice President

William Doud Packard
1861-1924
Secretary-Treasurer

Acknowledgments

This book covers the same territory the author wrote about in the first four chapters of the 1978 Automobile Quarterly publication "Packard – A History of the Motorcar and the Company", edited by Beverly Rae Kimes. However, the author concedes he was responsible for some errors while chronicling the Packard story 27 years ago.

In this book the author is making an effort to correct errors made and expand upon the history of the Packard Motor Car Company and the people who started it during the years before the move to Detroit. Since the author first wrote about this period more historical data has been uncovered and more information gleaned from the documents on hand.

One of the more important sources was the "Packard & Weiss" partnership ledger kept by W. D. Packard which, in great detail, shed light upon their activities during the first six months of 1900.

Most of the photos are from the author's collection and the G. L. Weiss collection which is now the property of the National Packard Museum in Warren, OH. There are 83 illustrations included in the book. Some new and many have been seen before in other Packard publications. Most are closely related to the text. Many photos in the author's and the Weiss collections were taken by the company for publicity purposes and have been widely disseminated.

The author extends special thanks to:

Wendell Lauth for his help with the early history and background of the Packard family and the city of Warren.
A. J. Balfour for his historical verification in certain areas where the facts were unclear. He also shed new light on the Model M, including original prints never before published. He deserves special mention for his proof reading – a job above and beyond the call of duty.
Duane L. Bohnstedt for his detailed copy of Ward Packard's list of Model Cs. The numbers helped the author to get a better count of Model B production.
Roger T. White for his information on the family background and life of George L. Weiss.

Additional thanks are due to:
Larz Anderson Auto Museum, Brookline, MA
The Studebaker National Museum, South Bend, IN

Willis Boyd–photo
Robert J. Neal – photos
Thomas G. Summers - photos
John A. Conde - photos
Richard Quinn - photo

Contents

Acknowledgements 6

Foreword 9

Chapter 1: The Packard Brothers 13

Chapter 2: George Lewis Weiss & The Winton Connection 27

Chapter 3: The Packard & Weiss Partnership 39

Chapter 4: The Ohio Automobile Company 65

Chapter 5: Henry Bourne Joy and the Detroit Investors 95

Chapter 6: The Move to Detroit 121

Epilogues 151

Appendix 161

Index 177

Foreword

One day back in 1977 I received a telephone call from my aunt, Edith Weiss Dingle, who resided in Cleveland, OH. She informed me that she had been contacted by a Mr. Terry Martin of Warren, OH, who was inquiring about her father, George Lewis Weiss, and his relationship with the Packard Motor Car Co. My aunt referred Terry to me in San Antonio, TX, where I was living at the time. This was the beginning of a great friendship that fueled my latent interest in Packard history and my grandfather's role as a co-founder of the company, along with James Ward Packard and William Doud Packard.

Terry was then involved in writing the opening chapters for Automobile Quarterly's wonderful book entitled "Packard – A History of the Motor Car and the Company", edited by Beverly Rae Kimes. In his research Terry had found many references to George L. Weiss in the Packard diaries and in other related historical documents, but there were many questions in need of answers. When I informed Terry I had a trunk full of patent papers, letters, photos, brochures, books and magazines— all relating to Packard and Winton history between the years of 1897 and 1903—he was elated. Within a few days Terry was on my door step and anxious to go over my treasure trove. We both soon realized how important these papers were for historians trying to fill voids, correct errors and flesh out the Packard story during the Warren years.

Luckily, my grandfather was a pack rat. He saved everything, and when he died in 1945 we found his papers packed into an old Navy Air Corps footlocker used by my father during World War I. Upon examination of the collection, Terry was able to learn more about these formative years and Weiss's role in them. The papers also added documentation to hearsay in many instances. One of the most interesting finds was a letter to Weiss from James Ward Packard suggesting they should start their own automobile company.

To be truthful, I had no idea of the importance of these papers until Terry came into the picture. Our family had moved to California in 1924 when my grandfather retired from the business world. My parents went along. I was two years old at the time. In 1925 we all moved to Beverly

Hills. Our house was only six blocks from my grandparents' home and we were together a great deal. During the 1930s, as I was growing up, I gravitated towards their home. My grandfather's shop was a special attraction. We spent many happy hours working on projects of mutual interest. Deep sea fishing was another pastime we enjoyed together when I could spare the time from school. Never during this period do I remember any mention being made of the Packard Motor Car Company, nor his role in it. In fact, I never saw the memorabilia he had tucked away in my father's footlocker until after World War II and he was gone. At this point, of course, I had many questions and it was too late to ask them.

After I became more knowledgeable about Packard history I began to realize what a mistake my grandfather had made when he traded his Packard shares for the Model L automobiles which he sold from his home in Cleveland, instead of retaining the stock as the Packard brothers had. They, like my grandfather, had somewhat of an adversarial relationship with Henry Joy, but they never let their emotions rule their decisions in regard to the stock. They seemed to realize that Joy had the money and the vision that eventually made the company a success, and they saw their Packard shares increase in value accordingly.

It is my opinion that in later years, when my grandfather came to realize the magnitude of the mistake he had made in selling his Packard stock, he became reluctant to discuss this period of his life. Nevertheless, he could not forget it and he must have realized the significance of the collection he had hidden from us for so many years. Thanks to his foresight it became possible for our family to donate his treasure to the National Packard Museum in 1999, on the one-hundredth anniversary of the founding of the Packard Motor Car Company.

Little was known about my grandfather's background or his involvement with Winton before these papers came to light. Even in some recent publications he has been described as a Winton "employee" and in one he was even said to have an engineering degree. Allegations which were wrong on both counts. George Weiss had a formal education which stressed accounting and he never worked for Winton. He was one of the initial investors in the Winton venture, however, and tried to encourage others to buy stock in the company.

Foreword

The confusion about his role with Winton and in the Warren years of the Packard story was corrected to a great extent by Terry Martin in the 1978 Automobile Quarterly Packard book which had in-depth coverage of the years before the move to Detroit. Without a doubt this publication is the most comprehensive history of the Packard Motor Car Company that has been written to date. To some it is referred to as the Packard "bible", and it enjoyed several successful printings.

Unfortunately, the Weiss collection didn't get to Terry Martin in time to make as thorough a study as he would like to have conducted. My grandfather's papers answered some questions but at the same time raised others which in turn required more study. The classic historian's dilemma! As press time loomed, research had to be curtailed.

In the last twenty-five years, Terry and other historians have continued to delve into the history of the Packard automobile during the Warren years. A lot has been learned from recently uncovered documents which shed light on the activities of the founders at the beginning of the century. A great deal of this new information came from the Studebaker Museum in South Bend, Indiana. They have a treasure trove of records relating to the Warren years and they have been very helpful to Terry, Jim Balfour and others by making their archives available to them. Other documents located since 1980 are: William Doud's "Packard & Weiss" partnership ledger and the board meeting minutes of the Ohio Automobile Co. After studying these informative papers, Terry found he had made some significant errors in his previous text, and Terry and I would like to have seen a revised edition of the A.Q. book published incorporating these corrections. Several years ago I spoke to Beverly Rae Kimes and asked about the chances of this ---- she said, "it was not to be". It was not considered to be economically feasible to modify or alter the text. Even though his text is to remain unaltered in the A.Q. book, Terry and I feel that, in the name of historical accuracy, he has an obligation to correct any mistakes and include new information that has come to light.

The purpose of this book is to revisit the Warren years covered by Terry in the 1978 Automobile Quarterly publication, expanding and correcting any known inaccuracies. In the process new information has been added which was previously overlooked. With the modifications, additions, and deletions it may seem to bear only a slight resemblance to Terry's original effort but all the historical events are included as they were before. Significant changes were made in regard to the partnership period (June 1899 to July 1900)—smaller changes elsewhere—all important from an historical standpoint. Both Terry and I want this revisit to the Warren years to reflect the best information from all sources available at this time.

Roger Turreff White

January 2006

Chapter 1
The Packard Brothers

The Packard family was well known in Warren, Ohio, many years before James Ward Packard and his brother William Doud Packard appeared on the scene and the Packard automobile became a reality. Samuel Packard emigrated from England on a ship named "Diligence" in 1638 and settled in West Bridgewater, Massachusetts. Many of his descendants moved west as the nation developed and opportunity beckoned over the horizon. Among those was John Packard. He was married in Philadelphia at the time of the American Revolution and moved westward to Washington County, Pennsylvania in 1780. Here his family of three sons and five daughters grew to adulthood. John Packard's second son Thomas came to the Connecticut Western Reserve in Ohio in 1801 and settled in Austintown Township in Trumbull County.

Thomas Packard married Nancy Ann Berry of Washington County, Pennsylvania, on January 28, 1802. Three months later, at the first meeting of the Youngstown Civil District he was elected supervisor of 'highways' for the Austintown area. On September 3, 1803, his first son, William Packard, was born. Thomas Packard's family would eventually include eleven sons and one daughter. Two sons would become judges, two were physicians, and another rose to the rank of brigadier general during the Civil War. Thomas Packard moved to Marshall County, Indiana, in 1835.

William Packard married Julia Ann Leach in Austintown on June 26, 1826. She was born in New Jersey and was a Mayflower descendant. Her father, Benjamin Leach, a blacksmith by profession, brought his family to Ohio in 1819. William and Julia Packard's second child, Warren Packard, was born on June 1, 1828. With their son and two daughters, the Packards moved to Lordstown Township in 1834. The following year William Packard became Lordstown's first postmaster. During the following sixteen years William fathered five more sons and two daughters.

In 1849 the Gold Rush began in California and it seems that William Packard could not resist the lure of riches. Along with thousands of others he severed his family ties and went west, never to return.

Warren Packard residence, 2 High Street, Courthouse Square, 1872.

Chapter 1 - The Packard Brothers

Three years before his father left for the gold fields in California, Warren Packard, age eighteen, started work at the store of Milton Graham, a pioneer iron merchant in Warren. The position was secured for him by his brother-in-law, Eli K. Wisell, who operated a carriage factory in Warren. Four years later he owned the Graham store and another which was in competition with him.

Warren Packard became involved in the local lumber business in 1861-1862 and eventually expanded his operations into Pennsylvania and New York. The Atlantic & Great Western Railroad was one of his principal customers. During the Civil War business was booming and this climate turned out to be advantageous for him.

In addition to the lumber business his interest in hardware continued and his involvement in this endeavor grew over the next two decades. Among his business partners were Rolla Barnum, Madison Cook, his brother B. F. Packard and James Brooks. The Packard & Barnum Iron Co. was started in 1865. They manufactured forged iron products including axles. By 1866-1867 a complete rolling mill complemented the steam forge and, early in 1867, the first merchant iron was being rolled in Warren. He was also involved with hardware stores in Greenville, Pennsylvania, with his brother John R. and his uncle Daniel Berry Packard plus another brother, Andrew J., in Youngstown.

For the rest of his life most of his business enterprises flourished. He soon became a leader in the Warren business community and acquired considerable wealth. In later years he became involved in real estate and the hotel business in Lakewood, New York, where he built a summer home on Lake Chautauqua.

Although his business interests were wide spread his home base was always Warren. He was a director of Warren Western Reserve National Bank and he maintained a large family residence on Warren's Courthouse Square.

In his personal life Warren Packard was not so fortunate. He married Sylvia Camp, daughter of Alanson Camp, a hotel proprietor, on September 1, 1852, and they had two sons. Their first son, Rolla, named after his business partner, died in 1855 at the age of ten months. A second son, Harry, was born in the fall of 1856. His mother died a few

W. PACKARD.   W. H. HULL.   SHELDEN MEDBURY.

PACKARD, HULL & CO.

Proprietors Franklin Foundry & Machine Works, on South and Liberty streets Warren, O. Manufacturers of Steam Engines, Portable upright Saw Mills, Bridge Bolts, and castings of all kinds. Repairing done on short notice.
August 15, 1866.

W. PACKARD.   M. W. COOK.   B. F. PACKARD.

PACKARD, COOK & CO.

Dealers in Iron & Hardware, Sign of the Broad Axe, Market Street, Warren, O.

W. PACKARD.   B. F. HIENER.   R. BARTHOLOMEW.

WARREN PACKARD & CO.

Builders, Manufacturers of Sash, Blinds, Doors, Flooring, Mouldings, Fence Pickets, Oil Tanks, Cisterns, &c., and dealers in Rough and Dressed Lumber, Shingles, and builders materials generally, at the Planing Mill, Canal St., Warren, O.
Aug. 15, 1866.

WARREN PACKARD.   B. H. BARNUM.

BARNUM & PACKARD.

Manufacturers of refined hammered Iron, Rail Road Axles, Mill Shafts, Piston Rods, and Forgings of all kinds, at the *Steam Forge*, Warren, Ohio. None but the best selected wrought scrap Iron used.   [Aug. 15, 1866.

Ad from the Western Reserve Chronicle
September 5, 1866

weeks later on December 4, 1856. She was only twenty-three. Harry died in December 1858, two months after his second birthday.

Warren Packard remarried on November 20, 1860, to Mary Elizabeth Doud. Mary was born in Warren on December 12, 1838, and spent her entire life in that city. She was the daughter of William Chapman Doud, a pioneer Canfield family. Her mother was Anna Paltzgroff of Lordstown whose ancestors came from Kutztown, Pennsylvania. They traced their German ancestry to the Rhine Valley region.

Warren and Mary Packard started their married life in a modest rented home at the corner of East Market and Elm Road. Their sons William Doud and James Ward Packard were born in that house at the time of the Civil War. William was named after his maternal grandfather while James received his name from James Ward of Niles, a prominent iron manufacturer in the Mahoning Valley.

The Packards owned a home on Courthouse Square at the time daughters Alaska and Carlotta were born. The property known as the Packard Block, built by James Ward Packard, occupies this site today. The family had built an imposing mansion on High Street by the time their daughter, Cornelia Olive, was born. It was in this house that the Packard brothers spent their teenage years with their three sisters.

Warren Packard died on July 28, 1897, and his second wife six years later on October 9, 1903. He had been a pillar of the Warren community and, fortunately, his sons had inherited his vision and work ethic. Now they were poised to make their own mark on the Warren business and industrial scene.

William Doud Packard was born in Warren on November 3, 1861. He was educated in the Warren public schools and he completed one year at Ohio State University. At an early age he showed interest in his father's business and took a position as bookkeeper and salesman in the family hardware store. He also learned telegraphy and became a telegraph operator when the store became an agent for the American Union Telegraph Company. Later he joined his father in the planing mill as the junior member of Warren Packard & Son.

The Packard, Cook & Co. hardware store on Market Street at Courthouse Square, c. 1867.

Chapter 1 - The Packard Brothers

James Ward, the younger brother of William Doud, was born on November 5, 1863. His mechanical aptitude appeared early in his life. After completing his primary and secondary education in the Warren public schools he went on to Lehigh University in Bethlehem, Pennsylvania, where he earned a degree in Mechanical Engineering in 1884.

James Ward began keeping a daily notebook during his college days. Although the entries were usually short and concise, these diaries were destined to provide the precise documentation historians would need to trace the development of the Packard saga during the Warren years.

Upon graduation from college in August 1884, James Ward took a position with the Sawyer-Man Electric Company in New York City, a pioneer incandescent lamp manufacturing concern which later would be taken over by Westinghouse. He started in the dynamo room at a dollar a day. Within a month he became superintendent of the dynamo operation and by November he was foreman of the mechanical department where he applied for the first two of the many patents he would earn during his lifetime.

James Ward stayed with Sawyer-Man for six years. During this period he gained a practical knowledge of the electrical industry and made many contacts that were to become important in later years.

William Doud had also worked for Sawyer-Man several years before his brother and had become acquainted with the business and the operation of the company. He was one of the first individuals to urge the city of Warren to build an electric generating plant. With a small generator set up at the Packard home he engineered several lighting demonstrations on the city street in front of city hall. The city's first power generating plant was built at the Summit Street location just west of Mahoning Avenue in 1890.

In 1890 James Ward returned to Warren and convinced his brother that they should start their own manufacturing operation which they would call the Packard Electric Company. William Doud had great confidence in his younger brother's mechanical and electrical abilities, and they both felt that their venture would be well accepted due to their father's stature in the community.

Fig. 5.—The Sawyer-Man Lamp Factory. (See Pages 1 and 2.)

Sawyer-Man Lamp Factory, New York, 1885.

Chapter 1 - The Packard Brothers

The official announcement of their new company appeared in the *Warren Tribune* on June 3, 1890. The headline read:

NOW IT'S ASSURED

PACKARD ELECTRIC CO.

THE NEWEST OF WARREN'S NEW ENTERPRISES

Part of the story went on to say:

"The contracts for two buildings, one of wood, 40 x 80, two stories in height, and one brick, one storey, 16 x 30, with a boiler shed, have been let. Work will be commenced immediately, and it is the hope of the proprietors that the machinery will be running by September".

The article continued by saying that the company was formed for the manufacture of "dynamos, lamps, and electrical specialties" and also mentioned that J.W. Packard would be president and W.D. Packard would be Secretary-Treasurer.

Two days later, on June 5, 1890, the official papers of incorporation were signed and the Packard Electric Company became a reality. From 10 employees at its inception, over the years, after it became a subsidiary of General Motors Corp., the number of employees grew to 13,000. Currently Packard Electric operates as part of the Delphi Corp. and is independent of General Motors. It is also interesting to note that the 40 x 80 two-story wood structure mentioned in the newspaper account was the birthplace of the Packard automobile.

Unfortunately, the stock offering for the new company was not taken up by Warren residents to the extent that the Packard brothers had anticipated and James Ward was obliged to call on his contacts in New York for financial help. To accommodate the new stockholders another corporation was formed on January 27, 1891.

The new entity was called the "New York & Ohio Co." and John W. Peale of New York was named president and James Ward, general superintendent. William Doud became secretary-treasurer of the new company as well, but in reality he wore many hats. It was here that he dedicated most of his efforts over the following years.

WARREN PACKARD & CO.,
MANUFACTURERS OF
LUMBER AND SHINGLES.

Branch Office, REED CITY, MICH. Proprietors of CITY PLANING MILL.

MILLS { SPRING CREEK, PA., BROKENSTRAW, N.Y., CHIPPEWA, MICH. }   Warren, O., Oct 30, 1883

Dear Ward. I have your of 26th. It is realy lucky isn't it that something turned up to make use for the little chaps. I have not answered as I was undecided what to say. Now it is settled and my mind is easy. It is all right. When you get a real soft snap take it of course. When you get to it write me all about it. How many of you. Who? And what did you see. All well

Hartily
W. P.

A note to Ward Packard from his father while he was still at Lehigh University.

The New York & Ohio Co. was created to manufacture incandescent lamps and transformers. All other manufacturing operations were carried out under the name of Packard Electric. William Doud traveled throughout the eastern states as the factory representative for the New York & Ohio Co., promoting Packard products to city-owned and private lighting companies. James Ward dedicated his attention to production and the improvement of the product lines. Nevertheless, his fascination for original work was soon to manifest itself in fields beyond lamp manufacturing.

It is not surprising that James Ward's vision led him to explore the various avenues of development relating to what was then referred to as the horseless carriage. However, he showed no interest in attaining this goal through steam or even electricity, both of which were being explored at the time. In 1892 he bought a naphtha launch for use at the family vacation home at Chautauqua Lake and maintained it himself. This, in all probability, was his first practical introduction to the internal combustion engine.

In 1895 the Europeans were far ahead of America in the development of the horseless carriage. To spur interest on the domestic front the *Chicago Times Herald* sponsored a contest that seemed to ignite intense activity among inventors with automotive interest. At this time the Packard brothers bought their first automobile, and William Doud made a trip to Europe and brought back information on various vehicles which were currently receiving attention on the continent.

Among them was the DeDion-Bouton tricycle that they purchased. According to James Ward it proved to be a thing of pain and sorrow. It was hard to start, made a lot of noise, was hard riding, and had faulty ignition and lubrication among other things. Still, although crude, it was an interesting machine and gave him something to experiment with and to improve upon. Most important of all it ignited his interest in the horseless carriage.

With renewed enthusiasm, James Ward subscribed to *"The Horseless Age"* a fledgling magazine devoted to the development of the automobile. On January 2, 1896, he engaged Edward P. Cowles as a "draftsman and pattern maker" to work at the factory but he didn't indicate what his duties were. On May 16th, however, his diary notes:

The Packard Electric Co. during the winter of 1893-94.

"Engage Cowles to work on motor wagon @ $12.00 per week 8 hours a day. Expenses to be divided between Howry, W.D. and J.W.P." J.H. Howry was president of the Packard Electric Co. Ltd. of St. Catherine's, Ontario, Canada, but it is not stated how he became involved with the project.

There was no further mention of the automobile project until January 1, 1897. When Henry A. Schryver, an expert machinist, who tended the manufacturing equipment for both Packard Electric and the New York and Ohio Co., noted in his daily log book that he prepared some drawings of a horseless carriage for JWP. Further notes indicate he worked on JWP's naphtha launch during the succeeding three weeks. It is of interest to note that Schryver later did most of the machine work on the first Packard in 1899.

Although it is well documented that 1896 was the beginning of JWP's work on a motorcar, there is no further mention of this work carrying on into 1897. Having learned all he could from the DeDion, James Ward discarded it. Eventually it was given to young Warren, W.D.'s son, as a plaything.

Ward was now ready for something more advanced to experiment with. His continuing interest in the horseless carriage was about to bring him into contact with Alexander Winton, a Cleveland bicycle manufacturer who was about to create his version of the horseless carriage.

The Packard brothers' interest in the Winton would also lead to their friendship with George Lewis Weiss, a principal investor in the Winton venture.

George Weiss in Winton Phaeton #4, Spring 1898.

Chapter 2
George Lewis Weiss and the Winton Connection

In 1895, one year before the Packard brothers bought their DeDion-Bouton, Alexander Winton, a Cleveland bicycle manufacturer built an experimental gasoline powered vehicle, which, although it was not a great success, kindled his interest in manufacturing a horseless carriage. On March 15, 1897, the Winton Motor Carriage Co. was formed to produce such a vehicle, and shares were offered on the open market.

Among the first investors was George L. Weiss, a man who represented several large railroad equipment manufacturers and also held a substantial portfolio in some of the more prominent ones such as Westinghouse Air Brake, Cleveland Forge & Iron and Butler Drawbar Attachment Co. The latter was a firm which at that time held the patent on the couplings which are still used today to join together most of the railroad cars in North America.

Weiss was a descendant of Dr. Johann Weiss, who emigrated from Walheim, Germany in 1740, and settled in Philadelphia. He married Rebecca Cox (January 8, 1749) and had 11 children, their first-born being Jacob Weiss, (September 1, 1750) who had the good fortune of obtaining employment with Benjamin Franklin in his printing business. He and Franklin developed a strong friendship despite their age difference.

In 1756 when Jacob was only six years old, Franklin had been in charge of a small military force sent to a wilderness area north of Allentown, Pennsylvania, known as the Lehigh Water Gap. The force had been organized to put down an Indian uprising after the massacre of Moravian settlers. Probably through Franklin, Jacob Weiss later became interested in moving to the area since the land was owned by the Moravian Church, his denomination.

Any resettlement plans Jacob may have had, however, were put aside at the onset of the Revolutionary War. Both he and Franklin became deeply involved in the conflict. Jacob Weiss received a commission as colonel in the Continental Army and served for two years as Adjutant Quartermaster General under General Greene.

After the war, Weiss visited the Lehigh Water Gap with renewed interest and purchased 700 acres of timberland from the Moravian Church. It was the same land where Franklin had built a fort some thirty-five years before.

In 1791 anthracite coal was discovered in the region and although Weiss recognized its potential, it was too far from the current markets to make mining economically feasible. Nevertheless, he formed the Lehigh Coal Mine Co. and had limited success. Transportation was the big problem. The region was mountainous and transport by wagon was too expensive for the coal to be competitive at any distance from the mine under normal circumstances. Efforts to use barges on the river were unsuccessful because the water was usually too shallow. By the 1820s it was decided that a canal could be built to make the river navigable. Jacob Cist, Weiss's nephew, became involved in the Lehigh Canal project that eventually opened the valley to the east coast markets.

During the early years of the nineteenth century Jacob Weiss brought German immigrants into the Lehigh Valley and founded the town of Weissport, Pennsylvania, followed by the town of Lehighton across the river. These towns grew as the mines prospered with the completion of the canal.

Col. Jacob Weiss died in 1838 and was buried on the hill overlooking Weissport. Although at the time of his death the family was fairly well off, it was his sons and his grandchildren who really benefited from the discovery of coal and lived comfortably off the proceeds of the mines into the 1880s.

Col. Jacob Weiss's grandson, Francis Weiss, made a fortune from mines in Eckley and Alden, Pennsylvania. Charles H. Weiss, a nephew of Francis and father of George L. Weiss, managed mining interests for his uncle for almost thirty years beginning in the 1860s.

George L. Weiss was born on February 19, 1862, in Allentown, Pennsylvania, where his mother's family lived. The family home, however, was in Eckley, Pennsylvania, where he grew up and attended school at the mines. He completed his education at the Mansfield Normal School in Mansfield, Pennsylvania, where he majored in accounting. His father Charles, in addition to administrative work at the mines, had an interest in a carriage manufacturing business in Lehighton and received a patent for wagon brake improvement in 1878.

By the middle 1880s the labor situation in the coal mines was making life not only difficult but dangerous. The mines had become a war zone. The Molly McGuires were fighting to organize the workforce in the mines, and Pinkerton Men were brought in to quell the riots. During this stressful period Weiss learned telegraphy and became the mine owners' principal contact with the outside world and the press when normal avenues of communication were cut off. The combination of labor strife and the fact that many of the mines were working out convinced Weiss that there was no future for him in Carbon County, PA.

In 1886 George Weiss moved to Cleveland, Ohio. Two years later he married Laura Lydia Turreff. Her father, William Fleming Turreff, was well established in the railroad equipment business as a representative of several major manufacturers. He took his son-in-law into the business and when he died in 1892, G.L., as his friends called him, carried on in his stead. Although Weiss was neither an engineer nor an inventor, he was well versed in mechanics. This knowledge was intimately intertwined with his railroad representations of mechanical and electrical equipment.

Weiss showed an interest in the horseless carriage early on. When Alexander Winton formed the Winton Motor Carriage Co. on March 15, 1897, to manufacture such a vehicle, he was one of the first investors. Weiss's representations kept him on the road much of the time, and he was in constant contact with some of the principal railroad leaders of the period. His son, Harold, related an instance when Diamond Jim Brady, the great promoter of the steel Pullman car, came to the Weiss home for breakfast with the family and G.L. asked Brady to show his son some of his diamonds. Where upon he removed the handle of his walking stick and poured a fairly sizeable collection of stones onto the table.

Weiss used his wealthy contacts in the railroad business to promote the Winton effort financially. Included with the collection of letters he received in 1897 were copies of the prospectus covering

The second Winton, a test vehicle, 1897. Alexander Winton is in the right front seat; George H. Brown, left front, with Weiss between them. Charles Shanks is in the back seat, left side. Tom L. Johnson is also in the back seat wearing a gray fedora and facing the camera. Johnson became mayor of Cleveland in 1901.

the original stock offering of the Winton Motor Carriage Co., and carbon copies of several letters he had written to friends telling them about his purchase of $5000.00 of Winton stock. In these letters he suggested that such an investment should also be profitable for them. Subsequent letters from George Brown, the General Manager of Winton, thanked Weiss for his efforts in promoting the stock sales and mentioned the progress of the firm's automobile production in general, and his car in particular.

An experimental Winton prototype had been built and tested that year with satisfactory results and a production model was in the works. One of the first publicity photos of the experimental Winton in 1897 pictures Weiss seated between Alexander Winton and George Brown, the plant manager, in the prototype outside the Winton plant in Cleveland.

The first production models of the Winton carriage did not appear until March of 1898. The first sale, recorded on April 1st, went to Robert Allison of Port Carbon, Pennsylvania. Weiss received Winton #4 on April 7th. No more sales were recorded until July 12th. It was a slow start, and to boost sales Winton launched a very determined publicity campaign under the direction of Charles B. Shanks, his publicist. Weiss was pictured in many of the early photos. One in particular, taken with his wife Laura at his side, was copied for magazine and newspaper advertisements. This ad became famous for its caption: *"Dispense with the horse"*.

In June of 1898, G.L. took Alexander Winton and George Brown, along with their automobiles, by train to the National Railroad Convention at Sarasota Springs, New York, where they exhibited and drove their cars, causing quite a stir. It is not known if any sales were consummated at that event but they generated considerable interest and excitement.

It is difficult to ascertain just where and when George Weiss and the Packard brothers first met, but their first documented meeting took place at a time when William Doud was spending considerable time at the Caulfield Hospital in Cleveland due to problems with his eyes. While in the hospital he undoubtedly heard more about Winton's venture and passed the information on to his brother. Still in the hospital on Friday, July 22, 1898, he recorded in his daily log: "Ward here at 10:30 to investigate the Winton Motor carriage – out riding with Mr. Winton". In

A 1898 publicity photo and article featuring Mr. and Mrs. Weiss in their Winton. The above advertisement uses the bottom photo.

Ward's diary on the same day he notes: "To Cleveland, tried Winton Motor carriage – fine price $1,000.00 – immediate delivery."

There was no mention of meeting Weiss during this visit to the Winton factory. A few days later, on August 4th, however, William Doud took a ride with George Weiss in his car. It is possible that William Doud had become acquainted with Weiss previous to this ride in his Winton. They both traveled extensively by train in conjunction with their sales efforts and it is certain both enjoyed the best of accommodations. The business world of the late 1890s was much smaller than it is today. Be that as it may, on Saturday, August 6th, Ward noted in his diary: "To Cleveland – went out with George Weiss in Motor carriage. Great! Ordered one from Winton Motor Carriage Co. $1000.00". Later that day Ward and his brother returned to Warren by train. Two days later Winton was paid a $200.00 deposit.

On August 13th, a week later, Ward went to Cleveland and took delivery of his new Winton carriage. It was a rough trip back to Warren. William Doud notes that the 65 mile journey took ten or eleven hours. He didn't arrive in Warren until 11:00 p.m. "Machinery broke down about 3 miles from home and he had to be towed in." Ward's notes were brief: "Went to Cleve came down in new motor carriage – hard trip, towed in. Winton carriage balance pd. 800.00."

Winton sold twenty-two automobiles in 1898. Ward Packard's car was #13*.

Apparently Winton wanted to please Ward because William Hatcher, the plant foreman, was dispatched to Warren the following Monday, August 15th, to repair the "motor" as Ward called it. By August 17th Hatcher had the engine running. Two days later it was placed in the stable in back of the Warren Packard house at 2 High St. where Ward made an arrangement with a Mr. Burns to take care of it, in much the same way as one would arrange to have a horse cared for.

* In many publications it has been stated that Ward received Winton #12, instead of Winton #13. The reason for this is that when Winton published his list of the first 50 Winton owners, he was so incensed by the desertion of Weiss to the Packard camp, that he eliminated Weiss's name and automobile (#4) from the original list, making the Packard purchase #12. Years later historians corrected the Weiss omission and the first fifty list increased to fifty one.

George Weiss and Alexander Winton at Steamboat Landing near Saratoga, New York, during the Railroad Convention, June 1898. Winton is in the driver's seat of the car, next to the edge of the road.

Chapter 2 - George Lewis Weiss and the Winton Connection

This was the beginning of a love-hate relationship between Ward and his Winton. Ten days after his traumatic trip from Cleveland, he took one of his Packard Electric stockholders on a 20 mile drive to Bloomfield and described the experience in his diary as "great". He continued to use the car during September and October without commenting on any significant problems. He obviously had continuing interest in the vehicle when he returned to the factory on November 17th, not for repairs but to get more information about the Winton operation.

During the first few months since Ward bought his Winton he must have been in contact with Weiss, for on November 30th he records that Mr. & Mrs. Weiss were in Warren and using his Winton during their visit. Ward returned to Cleveland on December 3rd and visited the Winton factory along with Weiss. During this visit they discussed the "failure of dynamo igniters" with Mr. Winton.

Problems continued into 1899. Ward visited the factory on January 2nd and Mr. Winton even went to Warren to see the car first hand on February 4th. He certainly was interested in the problems with his product and searching for answers. Part of Mr. Winton's interest in Ward's car was probably due to the fact that of the 22 automobiles sold in 1898, only the Packard and the Weiss cars had been sold to Ohio residents. Ward paid full price for his car, and he was not a stockholder as Weiss was. It is certain that his complaints were taken more seriously than those of George Weiss.

Ward made another visit to the plant on March 15th, then on March 28th Winton sent a man to Warren "to help put the motor together". But it seems his efforts were in vain. After three days the man left and Ward notes the engine is "very noisy and not running very well". On his next trip to Cleveland he discussed changing the engine but there is no record of this ever being done.

April 11, 1899, was the date Ward wrote to Weiss and intimated he was interested in manufacturing his own automobile and strongly implied that he wanted Weiss to be a part of the venture. Nevertheless, his struggles with the Winton continued even as he and Weiss were discussing their plans to enter into competition with Winton with their own motor carriage.

A production model of the Winton Phaeton sold in 1898.

Chapter 2 - George Lewis Weiss and the Winton Connection

After a difficult trip to nearby Niles, it was back to the factory on April 27th. He made the 8-hour trip with a friend in the Winton and had a difficult time keeping water in the radiator. They left the Winton and returned to Warren by train. The carriage remained at the plant until May 9th, when he picked it up but had to take the train home because of bad road conditions. He tried again on May 12th but "tyre" trouble delayed him in Ashtabula and he left the car with a Winton man to mount the spare. Finally, on May 14th a frustrated Ward notes in his diary "went to Ashtabula via Cleveland, left Ashtabula at 11:00 a.m. arrived in Warren at 3:30. One run away [horse] above Orwell, no one hurt." On June 10, 1899, Ward made his final trip to the Winton factory as a customer and "enjoyed supper and an evening with George Weiss".

It is probable that, during this final visit, Ward Packard suggested to Alexander Winton that he should make some modifications to his automobile. Winton was annoyed to the point that he said something like: "If you are so smart, why don't you build a machine of your own". Obviously, by this time Ward Packard and George Weiss had already come to the conclusion that they could do just that.

```
                                                    J.W. PEALE,
                                                       Prest.
                                                    J.W. PACKARD,
                                                       Vice Prest and Genl Mgr.
                                                    W.D. PACKARD,
                                                       Secretary and Treasurer.

                        MANUFACTURERS OF
                    THE INCANDESCENT LAMP
                    Packard   TRANSFORMER.

                                            MAIN OFFICE & WORKS,
                                              -WARREN, OHIO.
                    WARREN, OHIO.     April 11, 1899


Geo. L. Weiss, Esq.,
        75 Ingleside Ave.,
                Cleveland, Ohio.
Dear George,
            I endeavored to get you on the telephone this morning ,
intending if you were in Cleveland and could spare a few minutes
to run up today. I must go up sometime this week on business and I
hope that you will be at home. I am quite anxious to talk "horse" with
you. I have got Will making a special investigation on the other side
but have not had a report from him yet. I believe that this report
would be of some value to anyone contemplating starting into the bus-
iness here.  It is a branch of work which has a very great fascina-
tion for me and it is not impossible that I may go into it someday.
With this possibility in view I would like to talk matters over with
you. Kindly drop me a line and let me know whether or not you will be
at home the last of the week.
            With best wishes, I am,
    JWP-A240I.                          Yours very truly,
                                            J Ward Packard
```

The formation letter, April 11, 1899. James Ward Packard shows interest in the automobile as a business and approaches George Lewis Weiss as a potential partner.

Chapter 3
The Packard & Weiss Partnership
June 1899 – July 1900
MODELS: A, B, and C

When Ward Packard wrote to George L. Weiss on April 11, 1899, it was clear that he wanted to get into the motor carriage manufacturing business and was interested in having G.L. join him in the venture. He states in the letter: "I must go up [to Cleveland] sometime this week on business and I hope that you will be at home. I am anxious to talk 'horse' with you. I have got Will [his brother] making a special investigation on the other side [Europe] but I have not had a report from him yet. I believe that this report would be of some value to anyone contemplating starting into the business here. It is a branch of work which has a very great fascination for me and it is not impossible that I may go into it someday. With this possibility in view I should like to talk matters over with you."

Well before this letter was written, Ward obviously had been considering this idea quite seriously. He probably had discussed it with Weiss and he surely had discussed it with his brother sometime before he left for his "investigation" in Europe. The trials and tribulations he experienced with his Winton undoubtedly brought to light many areas where improvements could be made and a better product produced.

Ward and G.L. had become close friends through their mutual Winton experiences and Weiss seemed anxious to join him. On June 17, 1899, he sold his 170 shares investment in Winton stock for $12,000 – a $7,000 profit over the two years he had held it. On June 29th, after Weiss made a trip to Warren, Ward states in his diary that they had decided to put up three thousand dollars each if they could engage Hatcher.

William Albert Hatcher, known to his friends as "Bert", was born on December 31, 1871, in South Bend, Indiana. He only had an eighth grade education but he possessed an inventive mind, and he had become an accomplished draftsman and mechanic. At that time he was

Pages 10 and 11, Packard & Weiss Ledger, Job #357, 1899 entries.

a foreman at the Winton plant. It is interesting to note that both Ward and G.L. were so impressed with his abilities that their decision to proceed hinged to a great extent on securing his services.

It appears that Bert Hatcher wasn't overly happy with his position with Winton and he jumped at the opportunity to become part of the "Packard & Weiss" venture.

On July 3rd Hatcher made a written commitment to report for work on July 15th, for the purpose of developing "a practical motor vehicle, at the earliest possible date". The agreement also states "if the first machine proves successful, to immediately proceed with say six more sample machines for the purpose of development". The Packard brothers and Weiss agreed to furnish the necessary capital and to pay Hatcher $100 per month plus, "if a company is formed," $5000.00 worth of stock and the opportunity to purchase a reasonable amount of additional shares. In return Hatcher agreed to apply for any ensuing patents under the name of "Packard & Weiss"

It seems as if Hatcher was so enthusiastic about this new opportunity that he came aboard even sooner than planned, because on July 7th he had already completed the first drawings for the new carriage and was placed in charge of the New York & Ohio Co. drafting room. When the Packard brothers and Weiss entered into an agreement with Hatcher, it was planned to have all the work done in the New York and Ohio shops until new and separate facilities could be completed. In actuality "Packard & Weiss" and the New York & Ohio, Co. were two separate entities, each with their own set of books but operating under the same roof.

Ward Packard worked closely with Hatcher in the development of the new carriage but it was Hatcher's name that appeared on most of the drawings along with other New York & Ohio draftsmen from time to time. These included A.C. Nelson of Berea, Ohio, who became the second motor carriage draftsman on July 19th at $2.00 per day. They must have worked long hours committing their ideas to working drawings because on July 26th Ward notes that G.L. made a visit to Warren and was "well pleased with progress on the carriage".

William Doud Packard opened a ledger on August 5, 1899, recording all the income and expenditures during the period the "Packard

Number 1 Packard unfinished on the NY & Ohio shop floor. Note the two lever transmission.

& Weiss" partnership was in effect. Fortunately this ledger still exists and it, along with Ward's diary, provides us with a history of the partnership up to September 10, 1900, when the founders decided to reorganize as a corporation.

Fabrication of parts and orders to outside suppliers began the second week in August when payments were recorded in a account entitled "No 1 Carriage, Job # 357". Brightman Machine Co. and Cleveland Forge & Iron were among the first to be contacted, the latter, a firm with which G.L. had close business connections. Whenever it was feasible, however, the work was done in the shops of the New York & Ohio Co.

As the project progressed and their creation began to emerge, Ward sent Bert Hatcher to Cleveland to expedite the preparation of patterns, castings and forgings. Although G.L. was Ward's Cleveland representative for many business dealings in that city, Hatcher's presence was often necessary to resolve technical problems relating to the new vehicle. On October 30th the first engine was ready for testing and Ward noted "engine on new machine tests out at 7.1 h.p." This was lower than the expected 9 hp, and it is assumed modifications were made later to bring the horsepower up to the rating attributed to this engine.

On November 2nd Ward mentions the new machine shop was opened to separate the automotive work from that of the New York & Ohio Co., as well as his "last ride in old carriage" – he was about to replace his quirky Winton for "No 1 Carriage". Although the new machine shop was important from a production point of view, the big event of the year came four days later on November 6th, a snowy overcast day when Packard "Number One", the first Model A, was rolled out and driven for the first time. G.L. missed this initial trial but arrived the following day, November 7th, to see it in operation. Both the Warren *Daily Chronicle* and the *Warren Tribune* gave the event front page coverage although the latter mistakenly gave the credit for building the vehicle to William Doud instead of to Ward. Two weeks later, on November 22nd, "The Horseless Age", a magazine dedicated to motor carriage development, spread the word about the Packard "automobile" but also erroneously gave credit for the vehicle to Ward's older brother. It is of interest to note here the word "automobile" was finally coming into every day usage, replacing the terms "horseless" or "motor carriage".

Photo of the first Packard taken on November 7, 1899, the day George Weiss arrived to see it.

Chapter 3 - The Packard & Weiss Partnership

Weiss was delighted with the new vehicle and the decision was made to go ahead immediately with "6 to 8 more machines". In spite of this decision no more vehicles, or even parts for future production, were ordered until December 30, 1899. Nevertheless, work continued on No. 1. Although it was operative, Ward was still not satisfied with his creation. The transmission seems to have been one of the focal points of his attention during the waning months of the century, when his idea of the H gearshift pattern came to fruition. It was an idea that he patented and which was destined to become an industry standard for the first half of the 20th century.

By December 30th William Doud had recorded in the ledger that $2,189.72, in direct costs, had been charged to Job # 357 for the development of the new machine— and this didn't include Hatcher's salary. Still more would be spent on it during the coming months. Nevertheless, the partners seemed satisfied with their product. That same day Ward mentioned in his diary, "George Weiss and his father here, sign partnership agreement". This act formalized the July 3rd agreement the Packard brothers and Weiss had signed with Hatcher on that date and officially established "Packard & Weiss" as the Automobile Department of the New York & Ohio Co.

As 1899 was ending, the partnership was looking forward to building the new vehicles they had decided upon two months before. On December 30th they opened two new job orders to cover these vehicles entitled: "Eleven Motors - Job # 430" and "Eleven Automobiles - Job # 431". The job order for the engines remained open through May 5th and the automobile account wasn't closed until August 7th. These two job orders embraced all of the Model As and some Model Bs. The Model As were fashioned after No. 1, the prototype. All could be classified as experimental and all were slightly different. The first Packard was designed with a ram's horn-shaped front frame member supported by leaf springs, a design commonly used on horse-drawn carriages of the day. It was detailed on an August 14, 1899, drawing by Hatcher. On the same sheet he made an additional drawing, dated December 24, 1899, detailing the less complex straight-type spring support later used on the 1900 Model Bs. Nevertheless, photographs show at least three other Model As with the same rams horn suspension, the principal design feature used to differentiate the 'A's from the 'B's.

W. D. Packard seated in his Model A-21, the first car completed in 1900 and the second Packard built. Used as a test vehicle in April and May before he took possession of it as his personal car

Factory photo of W.D. Packard's A-21 "special" showing its elaborate wood body. This was the first production vehicle photographed with the single lever H style tansmission.

Chapter 3 - The Packard & Weiss Partnership

The first Packard, the 1899 prototype, was never given a number. As the new 1900 vehicles were nearing completion they were identified by motor numbers starting with A-21. The first automobile produced in 1900 was built for William Doud Packard, and assigned that number. It was completed in early April but payment for it didn't appear in the ledger until June 21st, probably because it served as a test vehicle, along with No. 1, for a couple of months before he took delivery of it. The body style was similar to its predecessor but the front axle was lower and it featured a rich looking wood dash with a brass rail adorning the top. Inside the dash was a compartment for storage of the crank, tools, and personal items.

G.L. received the second production car, A-22. According to the afternoon edition of the *Warren Daily Chronicle* it was shipped to him in Cleveland on April 13th and the ledger records a payment of $1,000.00 on April 20th. The same amount W.D. paid for his car. It was similar to the previous models but had a plainer dash, very much like those that appeared on the Model Bs a couple of months later. G.L. used this car as a demonstrator in his sales efforts in Cleveland where it was photographed in the 1900 4th of July parade.

Number A-23 had the distinction of being the first Packard sold to an outside party. Ward had previously noted in his diary that he had sold a "carriage" to George D. Kirkham on February 3rd when No. 1 was the only Packard operating. On May 2nd, Mr. Kirkham paid $1,250 for the vehicle and presumably took delivery close to that date.

George Kirkham was part owner of the Harris Automatic Press Co. in nearby Niles, Ohio. He had obviously espoused the merits of his Packard to his partners in the Harris family because the ledger records two more sales to family members in the same month. Packards A-24 and A-25 were sold to Charles G. Harris and Fred W. Harris on May 7th and May 17th respectively. The ledger clearly ties each of the first five owners with the motor number of the vehicle they received.

By April of 1900, one year had passed since Ward had invited G.L. to join him in the motor carriage venture. After almost six months of experimenting on Model As, the design of the Model B seems to have been decided upon. They now turned their attention to marketing their new product. On April 13th, the same day *The Chronicle* announced the shipment of Weiss's car, it also stated that the New York & Ohio Co.

Above: The third Packard, A-22, built for G.L. Weiss, shown here with his family during the 1900 Fourth of July parade in Cleveland.

Below: The same car at the factory in Warren prior to delivery.

would ship 6 more machines that month, and they had an equal number "under construction". There has to be some error in this report. The Packard & Weiss ledger indicates that only eleven 'A' and 'B' model vehicles were produced during the first seven months of 1900. The ledger only records six more sales, by payment date, after April 20th through July 11th, all to Warren residents. It is hard to tell where the 'A' models ended and the 'B's began because all the motor numbers had an 'A' prefix. The best estimate based on ledger entries, billing dates, and existing photos is that only the first five Packards produced (A-21 through A-25) were Model As. Additional confirmation is gleaned from G.L.'s note "June 1900. Shipped Mr. August Veghte his first automobile Packard — - same single seater as regularly manufactured at this time". On June 20th when August Veghte paid $1,250 for his vehicle with Motor # A-26, it was in all probability a Model B, the era of the Model A had ended.

Starting with motor number A-26 forward, the number-ownership relationship is not recorded but the chronological order of payments is very clear. Therefore, in the list of vehicles produced under the "Packard & Weiss" partnership motor numbers have been arbitrarily matched in that order in this book. An exception being motor number A-30, the Model B that George Blackmore purchased, probably in August, but not registered in the ledger and which is now the property of the author. The only other Model B known to exist has motor number A-39, invoiced after September 10, 1900. This car belongs to the National Automobile Museum in Reno, Nevada.

The "Packard & Weiss" partnership released information on the basic design of the Model B in April of 1900. That month the *"Horseless Age"* published an item under the heading of "the latest news from Warren" stating that the company "has been working for the past year developing and perfecting a gasoline motor vehicle – and [has] now commenced regular deliveries. They [started] out with a capacity of two carriages per week, which will be rapidly increased. We are promised photos and a complete technical description of the machine, which the company states is in no way experimental, in the near future. Numerous patents have been applied for, some have been allowed. Inventors are Messrs. Packard and Hatcher." On April 20th the *"Motor Vehicle Review"* published a similar announcement using almost the same phraseology.

During the development period of the Model 'A's both Ward and Hatcher were so busy that little time was devoted to filing for patent

George Kirkham with A-23 in front of his residence. The Packard, the fourth built, was the first sold to an individual outside the company.

A clearer photo of the Kirkham car in front of the plant prior to delivery.

THE FIRST ELEVEN AUTOMOBILES
(Job Oders #430 & #431)
April through September, 1900

Motor No.	Model	Paym't Date	Charged to	Price Paid	Remarks
A-21	A	June 21	W. D. Packard	1000.00	Completed in April — used as test vehicle 2 months before debited
A-22	A	April 20	G.L. Weiss	1000.00	Shipped to Cleveland — April 13th
A-23	A	May 2	George Kirkham	1250.00	First buyer outside the partnership Ordered February 3, 1900
A-24	A	May 7	Charles G. Harris	1250.00	
A-25	A	May 17	Fred W. Harris	1250.00	Invoice date May 8, 1900
A-26	B	June 20	August Veghte	1250.00	Pd 1000.00 down—Bal July 16, 1900
A-27	B	June 21	John F. McNutt	1250.00	
A-28	B	July 11	Al F. Harris	1250.00	Photo show B-style body
A-29	B	Aug 20	J.W. Packard	1250.00	From Packard and Weiss ledger
A-30	B	August ?	George Blackmore	1250.00	Current owner — Terry Martin
A-31	B	Sept 25?	Dr. S.P. Ecki	?	Delivered 3rd week in Sept. 1900

Pages 24 & 25 Packard & Weiss Ledger Job #431 Entries.

Chapter 3 - The Packard & Weiss Partnership

rights. It was not until January 16, 1900, that James Ward finally applied for his first automotive patent —- which wasn't issued until February 12, 1901. This and five subsequent patents awarded to Ward and Hatcher covered various parts designed for the first Packard automobile of 1899. Among these was the automatic spark advance and the H pattern gearshift which became the industry standards. The latter, granted patent No. 912928 on November 4, 1902, was used on most cars worldwide up to the advent of the automatic transmission. The automotive spark advance is still in use on many internal combustion engines. Also, although it was not patentable, Packards were the first automobiles to make use of a foot pedal for speed control.

In May of 1900 a prototype of the Model B must have been assembled because a news release with photos was sent to various publications. They quaintly described the Model B as follows:

> "It is solidly built, to endure high speeds on rough roads, and the workmanship is thorough and first class. The wheels are 34 in. in diameter, with 3 in. pneumatic tires – The frame is of seamless steel tubing, made flexible by ball joints – Double elliptic springs support the body at the rear, and a reversed elliptic spring carries the front end."

> "The engine is of the horizontal, single cylinder, four cycle type, with a [throttle] control. [It] is designed to run at a maximum of 800 revolutions, and at this speed, it will brake [at] 9 h.p. All ordinary grades can be climbed [in high] gear. A spring transmission is interposed between the engine and the gear shift, which prevents binding in the bearings and relieves the wheels of the 'kick' of the explosion. A gear and chain drive is used. The reverse is a [low gear], [allowing] with [various] speeds of the engine, from 6 to 10 miles per hour".* "The hill climbing [low] gear is approximately the same [ratio] – the speed of the engine [being] controlled by a pedal operated by the right foot of the driver. The two forward speeds, reverse, and the brake, are controlled by a single lever, in the right hand of the driver. Any one of these operations can be performed instantly, -if the brake has been applied and it is desired to [shift] into

*Recent experience by the author, with *Old No. 1*, make it clear that it would be impossible to reach these speeds in reverse and still retain steering control.

Model B (A-28) purhcased by Al F. Harris on July 11, 1900. Photo taken in front of the plant of the Harris Automatic Press Co., Niles, Ohio.

George Blackmore standing beside his Model B (A-30). This car is currently owned by the autho

Chapter 3 - The Packard & Weiss Partnership

higher [gear], it is not necessary to pass through the [low gear], which, if the carriage was running, would make [for] a very unpleasant, if not dangerous, [reduction in] speed. Steering is done by a lever in the left hand. In addition to the hand brake, a powerful foot brake, acting on the rear axle is provided. The chain is a, special nickel steel, roller chain which, under the most severe tests, has shown no appreciable wear and [has] an ample margin of strength."

"The body of the carriage shows the best possible coach work and upholstering, and the aim has been to get rid of the 'horse wanted' appearance. The leather dash is not used, but instead a boot or box forming part of the body. In this is ample space for parcels, waterproofs, etc. The mudguards are ample and designed more with a view to utility, rather than carriage appearance. A complete outfit of all necessary tools, wrenches and oilers is supplied with each machine. A chime foot bell is fitted and a single special automobile lamp is affixed to the center of the front spring".

"All machines are given a thorough test before they leave the factory. [With the testing apparatus] the rear driving wheels of the machine under test are supported on a pair of endless belts running over pulleys on two parallel shafts. One of these shafts is provided with a brake pulley by means of which any desired load can be applied. A tachometer is attached to the engine, indicating at all times the exact speed, and while on this tester numerous [readings] are taken from each engine. The machine is run under varying loads and speeds for one or two days [and is then] taken out for a further, and final, test on the road. Thus, when the highly finished body of the carriage is fitted, all of the mechanism has been thoroughly tested and is in perfect running order".

Since George Weiss was making every effort to sell Packard automobiles in Cleveland, Ward was anxious for him to have a Packard with an engine which was up to date in every way. On May 9th he wrote to Weiss to say he had just received a lighter pair of flywheel springs and was sending them to Cleveland, along with a man to put them on. (These springs took the shock of the piston firing, the transmission and the crankshaft not being directly connected). They were learning

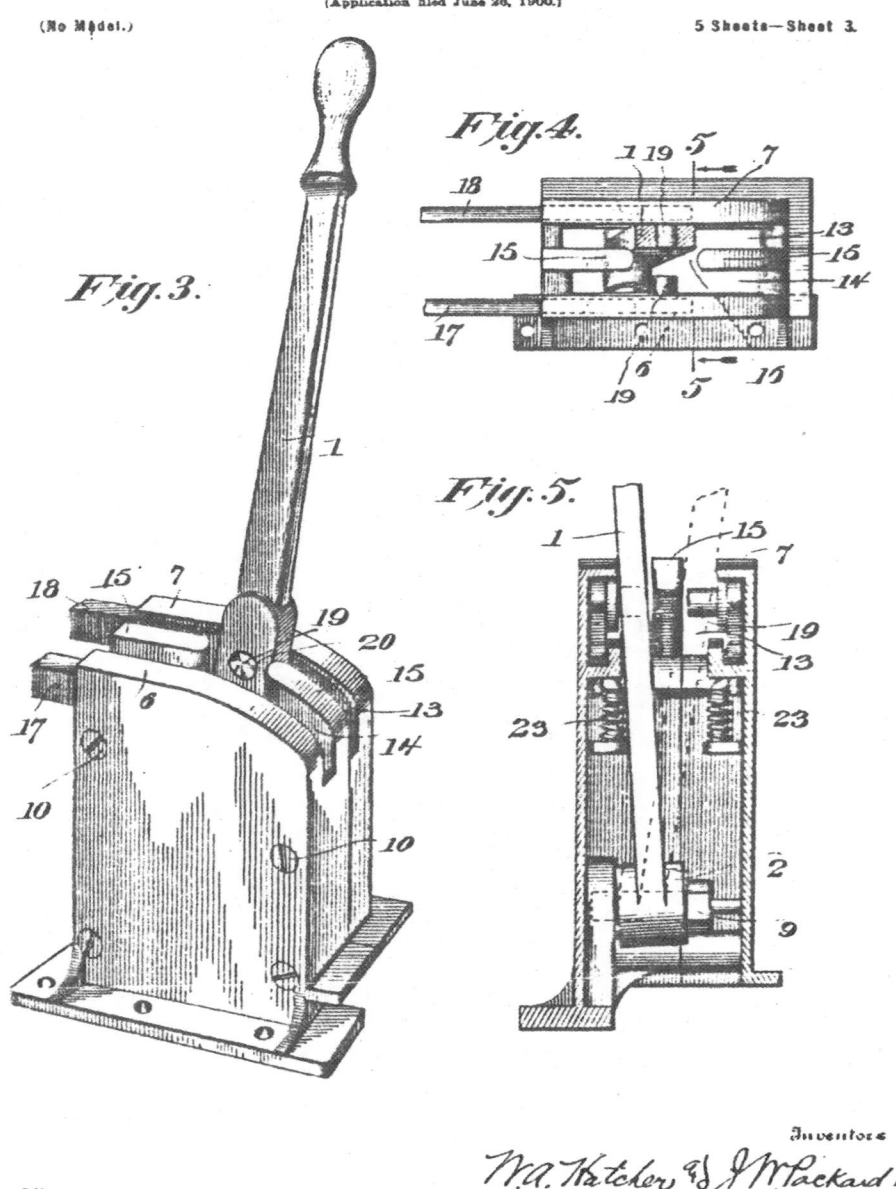

The first automotive transmission control with an 'H' pattern configuration.

Chapter 3 - The Packard & Weiss Partnership

something from the carriages in use and Ward commented to G.L. that he was "pleased to say that nothing has proved radically wrong or weak!"

In the same letter Ward said " We are getting along very well in the shop now and within two weeks we will be ready to order material for 24 more carriages". Unfortunately, it is not known exactly when these materials were actually purchased because the related entries do not appear in the "Packard & Weiss" ledger. They definitely were not included in account # 431 with the first eleven automobiles. But Ward's statement clearly indicates his intent to double production.

With the output of the Model Bs going well, Ward and G.L. began to see the need to publicize their Packard automobile. They wanted to prove to everyone just what their product could do. They decided that this could best be done with public endurance tests. On Saturday morning, May 26th, they left Cleveland bound for Buffalo, New York, in the Weiss machine (A-22), stopping in Ashtabula that morning and in Erie, Pennsylvania for dinner. The roads were found to be generally good and the car hit speeds of up to 22 miles per hour at times. They encountered no trouble during the 13 ½ hour run, even though the final 30 miles were made after dark on roads which were not familiar to them. They arrived in Buffalo so dusty and dirty that they were almost refused accommodation in one of Buffalo's better hotels. Nevertheless, after explaining that they were not on a pleasure trip but were involved in testing the long distance capabilities of their vehicle, they were finally admitted.

Sturdy construction and reliability on long trips such as this became the Packard trademark. In fact, the heavy tubular construction of the chassis, which was fastened to the front axle with ball joints, proved to be a problem. Due to the lack of flexibility, when one front wheel fell into a hole the other would be raised in such a manner that the spade handle on the steering tiller might be pulled from the driver's grip.

Warren's first automobile accident occurred because of this problem. Charles Harris was the victim, along with his passenger John McNutt, who also was a Packard owner. The Warren newspapers carried the story that on June 21st. Harris was driving from Niles to Warren and "while rolling along at a fair speed a rut in the road jolted the machine and jerked the steering lever from Mr. Harris' hand". The automobile swerved into a ditch and passenger McNutt was thrown from

A Model A chassis on the factory test stand which had an unpainted removable body to accommodate the operator.

the vehicle and suffered a sprained ankle. Mr. Harris escaped injury but the Packard did not. It was rather badly in need of repair.

In spite of the heavy workload related to the development and production of the 'A' and 'B' models, Ward and G.L. were contemplating the need for a new and more powerful Packard. On March 17th, even before William Doud's A-21 was completed, they opened a new ledger page entitled "Special – GLW & JWP – Job # 435". This account registered the direct costs for the first two Model C's. For two months there wasn't much activity in the account but on May 14th Ward wrote to G.L. alluding to "nickel steel" which he had ordered "for use in our two special 12 H.P. carriages". From that time forward, the activity in the account picked up and it continued at a brisk pace throughout the summer months. By July they had their "special" ready to introduce to the public. The August 28th issue of the "*Motor Vehicle Review*" called it "the new racing machine" by virtue of its more powerful engine. But in appearance it was similar to the Model B.

In the course of the development of the first two Model C's, Ward realized the need for some extra help in the engineering department and contacted the Case School in Cleveland. They recommended a recent Mechanical Engineering graduate by the name of Russell Huff. He was hired, started work on July 1, 1900, and soon became an important member of the engineering team. Huff stayed with Packard for many years, eventually becoming the head of the engineering department after the move to Detroit.

During the Warren years, the Packard automobile underwent many changes in body styles and models within the same calendar year. The first bodies, spanning Models A and B, were all built by Morgan and Williams, a local buggy manufacturer located just a few blocks from the Packard plant. All of the chassis were produced in-house. Lot sizes varied from 5 to 20, allowing the company ample time to experiment with the first examples from each lot and then incorporate improvements in the following series. It should be noted that all of the one cylinder engines built in Warren were designed by Bert Hatcher. All the nine horsepower engines used in the Model As and Bs were essentially the same, although many improvements were made when the need was perceived.

Two photos of one of the two experimental Model C's taken on the same day in the fall of 1900. Ward Packard is shown seated in the driver's seat in the top photo.

Chapter 3 - The Packard & Weiss Partnership

The George L. Weiss Model C Special in front of his home on Ingleside Drive, Cleveland, Ohio. Only two Cs were completed in 1900. Ward Packard received an identical automobile. One of these vehicles was subsequently sold to Mr. W.D. Sargent, president of the American Brake Shoe Co., Chicago, Illinois.

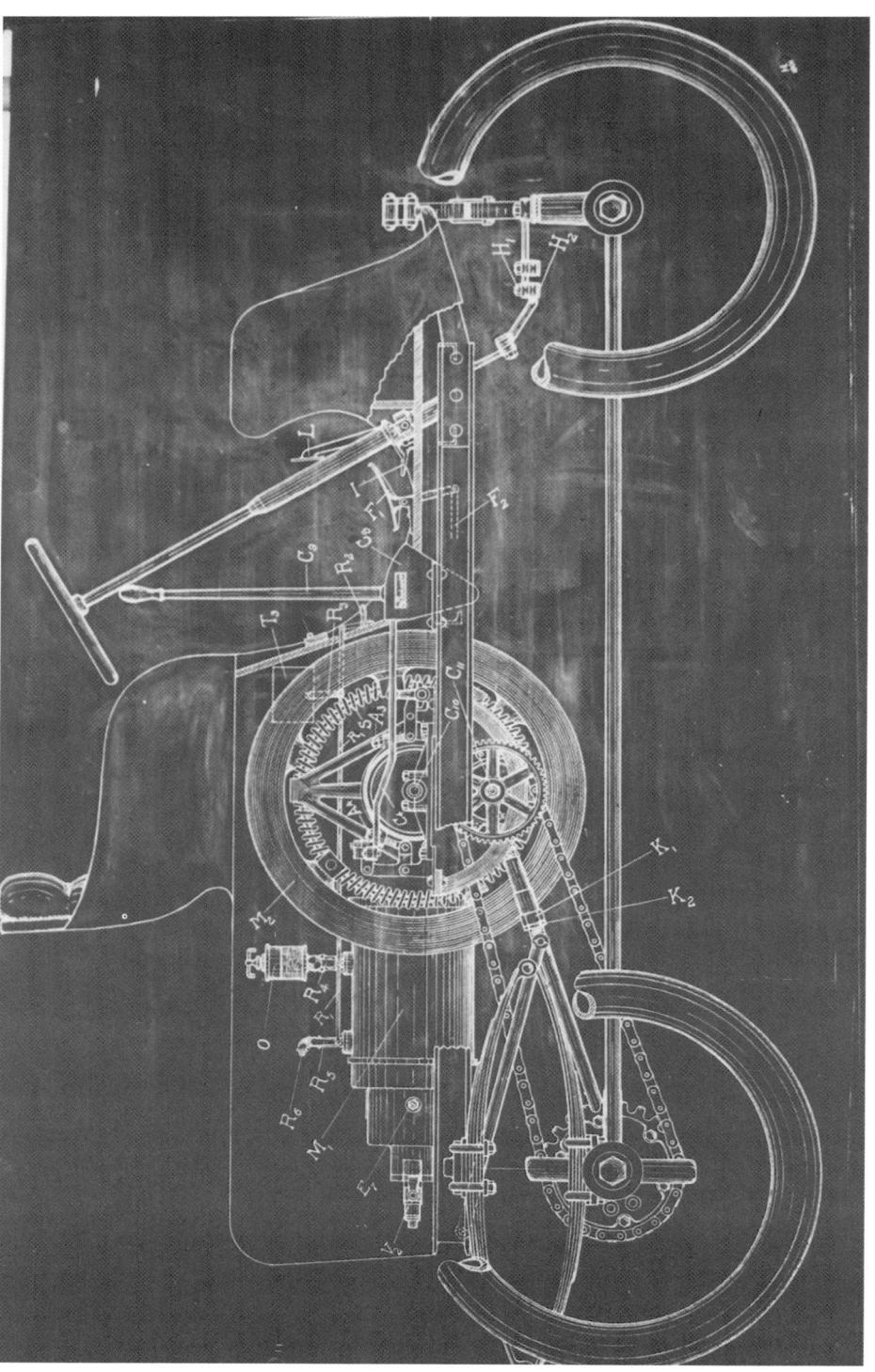

Large scale drawing of the Model C on a board in the drafting room.

Chapter 3 - The Packard & Weiss Partnership

By the summer of 1900 the "Automobile Department" of the New York & Ohio, Co. was expanding rapidly but W.D.'s ledger made it clear that expenses were exceeding income. Each partner had already paid in funds in excess of their initial $3,000. It was obvious that they needed to find additional investors. In a letter Ward wrote to G.L. on August 29th he mentioned having written to Adolph O. Kreiger, a representative of the Daimler Works, a European firm he felt might be a source of investment capital. His comment was "I would just as soon have German money as any".

Five weeks before this letter was written, July 20, 1900, the partners had decided that incorporation was the solution to their problems. They hoped it would provide them with the funds they needed to expand their operation through the sale of shares in the company. They had been discussing this among themselves and with the principals of the New York & Ohio Co. since May. Now, being of one mind, the Packard brothers, George Weiss and J. W. Peale, an officer and stockholder of the New York & Ohio Co., sat down together to restructure the "Packard & Weiss" partnership. An organizational change was coming that would strengthen the company and facilitate future growth.

An artist's imaginary aerial view of the factory, ca. 1902.

Chapter 4
The Ohio Automobile Company

The founders' vision for the future was limited under the provisions of the "Packard & Weiss" partnership, operating as the "Automobile Department" of the New York & Ohio Co. This arrangement was causing administrative difficulties. July found the partners committed to the idea of forming a new company under the laws of West Virginia, which offered advantages not available under Ohio law. On September 10, 1900, documents were signed establishing the "Ohio Automobile Co." under which Packard automobiles would be manufactured and sold until October 13, 1902. The sum of $100,000 in capital stock was subscribed, $10,000 being paid in, and the company had the privilege of selling additional shares and to increase capital stock to $500,000. Share certificates of one hundred dollars each were awarded as follows: James Ward, William Doud Packard, thirty-three shares each; George L. Weiss, thirty-two shares; James P. Gilbert (a Packard Electric stockholder), one share; William A. Hatcher, one share.

The first stockholders meeting took place on October 24, 1900, and during this meeting James Ward was elected president and chairman of the board, as well as general manager. George Weiss was named vice president, and William Doud, secretary-treasurer.

The partners were now becoming convinced that their company had a bright future. While they were contemplating their reorganization they produced their first piece of promotional literature, a four page leaflet describing the Models B and C, and expounding the company philosophy in regard to their product. *"The Horseless Age"* published the leaflet verbatim in their October 3rd issue and described it "as a model of business literature". The partners were so pleased with the editor's response that they purchased one half and full-page ads in subsequent issues of the same magazine.

Before wide spread promotional efforts were started most of the sales were concentrated in Ohio and the Midwest. The first owners had been made aware of the auto's existence by friends and other Packard owners. Now the Automobile Club of America was about to provide the company with a completely new avenue by which they could promote and display their product in the lucrative northeastern market. In April of 1900 the Club let it be known that from November 3rd to the 10th that year

An early advertisement of the Ohio Automobile Co., illustrating both Model B and C carriages.

Chapter 4 - The Ohio Automobile Company

Five early Packards — left to right: one Model A, 2 Model B's, and two Model C's. This photo with background eliminated was used in the company's first advertisement in The Horseless Age, November 7, 1900.

Goerge L. Weiss and his wife, Laura, in their Model C Special in front of their home on Ingleside Dr., Cleveland, Ohio.

Chapter 4 - The Ohio Automobile Company

t would sponsor the first National Automobile Show in Madison Square Garden. New York City beckoned and the Ohio Automobile Co. was determined to be present.

Without a doubt, the wealthy were the only buyers of automobiles at the turn of the century and the purchase of a particularly prestigious vehicle within the well-to-do social set often led to additional sales. The Packard presence at Madison Square Garden was essential to spur East Coast sales.

Packard went to the automobile show with a vengeance. George Weiss was in charge of the company exhibit. Two cars were displayed inside, the Model B (Standard) and the Model C (Special). The latter, Weiss's car, had a steering wheel, a novelty at the time, whereas most of the other vehicles featured lever steering systems. Besides the two models on the floor Weiss stationed two more outside, giving demonstration rides to prospective buyers. William D. Rockefeller certainly noticed. He bought two cars and became a great Packard booster. Boston's Hollis Honeywell was intrigued as well and bought one of the cars on display. These two sales to social leaders were significant since they set a pattern for Packard promotion and merchandising to this segment of society for many years to come.

During the show Weiss carried out the promotional efforts for the company. In addition to his sales role, Weiss handled all contacts with the press. In answer to inquiries by reporters he was quoted as saying: "We have no million dollar factory, but are turning out thoroughly practical road vehicles for delivery, which is more than many who are making bigger claims are doing. Our desire in bringing out a gasoline motor vehicle has not been an endeavor to make anything radically new or especially light and cheap, but has had in mind the attainment of perfect service on ordinary American roads".

It was Weiss, incidentally, who would be doing most of the traveling for the company and setting up dealerships. Ward, of course, did attend shows but preferred staying in Warren. He was a quiet man whose basic interest was in research and development, not sales and marketing, Weiss's forte.

The Packard cars made a splendid showing at Madison Square Garden, and the event was a milestone for the company. The Packard

The 1902 Model F as it evolved with a longer chassis and front radiator. This photo was taken in Cleveland with chauffeur Chaffee at the wheel and Bert Hatcher at his side. Weiss is in the back seat on the right side. The gentlemen in the other seat has not been identified.

automobile was now attracting national recognition. Four days after the show closed the company made arrangements to open an eastern sales office of the Ohio Automobile Co. at 114 Fifth Avenue, New York City. It was managed by George B. Adams and the New York office was an instant success. The first production Model C – with motor number fifty-six – would be sold to Charles C. Otis of Yonkers. Fifteen of the next Model C's would go to New York State residents.

By early January 1901, the Ohio Automobile Co. had over $40,000 in orders on hand. This amounted to thirty-three cars, a number that could not be handled by the small work force. A concerted effort was made to recruit qualified personnel, and machinists from all over Ohio answered the call. The company was offering 25 cents per hour for machine work, and 27½ cents for work on the production floor day or night.

Outside of Ohio some very influential people were being drawn to the Packard banner. Albert R. Shattuck, president of the Automobile Club of America and partner in one of the East's most prestigious automobile sales organizations, H.B. Shattuck & Son of Boston, was one of them. On March 27th, he sent his representative, Ben Smith, to Warren, and George Weiss promptly assigned to the Shattuck enterprise the right to sell Packards throughout the Northeast. On June 15th Shattuck entered a twelve-horsepower Packard in the first annual race meet of the Automobile Club of New England at the Brookline Country Club. Two weeks later he opened a second showroom in Newport, Rhode Island. Shortly afterward William Doud visited him, first in Boston where both he and Smith complained that they weren't getting Packards as quickly as they thought they should, and then in Newport where Shattuck picked him up at the railroad station in an electric carriage to drive the point home. All he could do at the time was to explain that they were a small company and they were expanding as quickly as they could.

By early spring of 1901 George Weiss arranged to have Alden S. McMurtry join George B. Adams as a partner in the New York office at 114 Fifth Avenue. Together they formed the Adams-McMurtry Co., investing their own funds, and became the exclusive dealers of Packard automobiles in New York State. Although they were referred to as Packard's Eastern Department, they were financially independent of Warren, and they operated as though it was a branch of the factory until

James Ward Packard in E-71—The only Model E ever built.

Chapter 4 - The Ohio Automobile Company

October 18, 1902, when they sold their company to the Packard Motor Car Company. After the sale Adams stayed on as Eastern Department Manager for several months.

McMurtry visited Warren on April 26th and drove to Cleveland with Ward. At the time of this trip, according to Ward's list of motor numbers and owners, McMurtry ordered C-70 "special". The very next order listed by J.W. is Model E-71, the only automobile ever mentioned with an "E" designation. Evidently McMurtry decided not to take this car and Ward lists himself as the buyer, adding that it was a "special carriage all around. Practically all parts different from others". Ward's list explains the Model E mystery, but what happened to the Model D? Nowhere in the known Packard records is there any reference to a "D" Packard.

James Ward Packard described the Model E-71 as an entirely different experimental Model F built for his own use. His description of the vehicle was published in the August 13, 1902, issue of the *"Horseless Age"*. They said it looked like a standard F with the exception of a custom rear seat and two acetylene headlights for night driving. The following excerpt from their article relates some of this experimental model's newer features:

> "A new departure in this vehicle is the adoption, after a long series of tests, of 2 inch hollow steel axles, running on bearings consisting of 7/8 inch steel balls. Each axle has a 1-inch hole running through its entire length. The hub brakes are of new design, double acting and very powerful, [and there is] a very effective single acting brake on the end of the transmission shaft, operated by throwing the clutch lever forward. The transmission is the same as on the [standard] model 'F', giving three speeds ahead with [only] two gears in mesh at any time, plus a reverse.

> "The carburetor is of the float feed pulverizing type, and one [setting] gives a uniform mixture for all variations of engine speed. The fenders are of aluminum, painted and striped to match the body. The steering is by worm and segment, with a special cushioning device for relieving the worm of the shocks produced on the wheels by bad roads".

Around the time of the McMurtry visit, the factory was beginning to deliver many of the presold cars. A large number of sales were now

1902 Model F's in storage at the factory. Winter production, mostly sold, awaiting delivery to their owners in the spring.

Chapter 4 - The Ohio Automobile Company

going to the Northeast, and in this area it was a common practice to put a car on blocks during the months when driving was less than pleasurable. Therefore winter deliveries were seldom made, and more often than not the factory was expected to store the car until the new owner desired it. Spring, therefore, was a profitable period for the Packard plant, the stored cars were being shipped out and paid for, bringing in much needed cash and relieving the pressure on the already limited production facilities. (Normally only down payments were received with new orders).

On April 30, 1901, at the stockholders' meeting the partners decided to reduce the 5,000 shares ($500,000), allowable in the company charter to 2,500 shares ($250,000). The reason for this is not stated in the minutes of the meeting. It is not known how many shares had been sold at that date but it is possible that they did not think it was wise to have such a large amount of unsold shares on the company books when they were offered for sale on the open market.

The Ohio Automobile Company was now growing at a steady pace but it had very little it could call its own. It leased the buildings of Packard Electric and used the machinery of the New York & Ohio Co. At the stockholders' meeting on September 30, 1901, some big changes were made. It was decided that the buildings of Packard Electric would be purchased by the Ohio Automobile Co. for $13,000 in cash. This included the original building built by Packard Electric and its addition in 1891. It was also decided to buy additional land next to the existing plant from Jacob B. Perkins to facilitate further expansion. The stockholders also accepted an offer from the New York & Ohio Co. to purchase all the machinery, tools, and fixtures presently being used by the Ohio Automobile Co. for $15,602.02. Packard automobile operations would now stand alone.

That same afternoon, it was also concluded that all business credits and obligations of the "Packard & Weiss" partnership would be assumed by the Ohio Automobile Co. The stockholders further authorized the issue of fifty-shares of capital stock to William Hatcher in accordance with the terms of the "Packard & Weiss" agreement of July 3, 1899. Five patents applied for under the same agreement were also transferred for the sum of $30,000 – or three hundred shares of stock, one hundred each to W.D. Packard, J.W. Packard and George Weiss. Both Ward and G.L. also received twenty-five shares of stock ($2,500)

James Ward Packard in a Model C before the start of the New York to Buffalo endurance run. George L. Weiss shared the driving with Packard during the event.

each for their work during the two previous years, neither of them having been paid up to that time for their efforts. During these initial years it was James Ward who developed the automobile that carried his name, along with considerable help from Bert Hatcher. It was also Ward who spearheaded and developed the production process. Weiss, as vice president, was the sales and marketing arm of the company. He traveled widely in this role, established agencies and publicized the virtues of the Packard automobile. William Doud, as secretary-treasurer of both the New York & Ohio Co. and Packard Electric, found that the administration of these companies required most of his time now that his brother was so deeply immersed in the automobile venture. Consequently, he reached a point where he devoted only incidental time to the automotive side of the business.

The minutes of the Ohio Automobile Co. record that as of September 30, 1901, 760 shares of the company had been sold, mostly to the founders, friends and family. While this demonstrated their confidence in the company and its future, they realized the need to attract outside capital. Doing this required publicizing the Packard name and the quality of their automobile.

The lack of reliability was an inherent problem for most automobiles at the dawn of the new century, and endurance runs became a stage for manufacturers to prove the mettle of their product. In September of 1901 the Automobile Club of America sponsored a six-day run from New York to Buffalo. The run was to end at the site of the Pan American Exposition then in progress. The event proved to be a triumph for the Packard automobile and garnered an immense amount of publicity for the company.

Five Packards were entered in the event, three by the Ohio Automobile Co. One was driven by Ward Packard along with George Weiss, another by William Hatcher and Packard chauffeur Charles C. Chaffee, and a third by A.L. McMurtry, representing the New York office. The privately entered Packards were driven by Dr. T.J. Martin who took Buffalo Packard dealer Ellicott Evans along as a passenger, and John M. Satterfield who traveled alone. It is interesting to note that the McMurtry car was registered as being a fourteen horsepower vehicle and the Martin car as a sixteen horsepower. Packard buyers during this period were offered a choice of horsepower running from nine to twenty- four.

William A. hatcher at the wheel of a Model C prior to the New York to Buffalo run. Charles C. Chaffee, the chauffeur, is seated next to him. They shared the driving during this event.

Chapter 4 - The Ohio Automobile Company

The purpose of this contest of 390 miles, over roads seldom traveled by automobiles, was to prove that American manufacturers were producing the best automobiles for American roads – which, incidentally, were notoriously bad. Of eighty starting entries only five were European makes, and only two of these finished – both were Panhards. One of these cars was driven by David Wolfe Bishop and the other by Albert R. Shattuck, the Boston Packard dealer who also sold other makes through his family company, H.B. Shattuck & Son. Fifty-four of the entries were gasoline powered automobiles and twenty-six were steamers. Sizes ranged from a 78 lb. motor driven bicycle to a 10,189 lb. steam truck. The Packards were competing in Class C, 2,000 lbs. and over.

On the Wednesday before the event began the Ohio Automobile Co. shipped its cars to New York. James Ward, George Weiss and William Hatcher were all present two days later to look over the competition, and socialize with the contestants over the weekend. Not since the Madison Square Garden show had so many motor vehicles been gathered together in one place in America.

On Monday, September 9th, at 8:00 a.m., the vehicles started up Fifth Avenue with appropriate fanfare. When the smooth streets of the city were left behind the troubles began. Getting lost was just one of them. Around Tarrytown the sand was eight to ten inches deep and it often covered stones that severely jolted both vehicles and occupants. The hazards were many - loose planks on bridges, steep grades, and at times the ordeal of getting around stalled cars. But all five Packards made it to Poughkeepsie, the layover for the night.

The second day, during the run to Albany the Panhard drivers and others decided to turn the endurance run into a race – something the organizers had feared. The Victor steamer turned over, injuring the driver and resulting in the total loss of the machine. The Packard team resisted the temptation to race. Those who participated in the racing received reprimands at the control point. With the exception of the Panhards, the foreign machines seemed to be shaking themselves apart. The Packards were doing well, except for a minor problem on the Satterfield car. Others were not so lucky. One reporter noted the number of problems the gasoline vehicles suffered seemed to be in direct proportion to the number of cylinders the engine had. This must have strengthened Ward's resolve to stick with the single-cylinder engine. He was always leery of multi-cylinder engines.

A 1901 Panhrad Levassor, belonging to Albert Shattuck, the Boston Packard dealer, who also represented other companies. This photo taken September 8, 1901, before the start of the New York to Bullafo run shows Albert Shattuck standing on the right side of the car. Also shown in this photo are George L. Weiss standing behind the car with his arm resting on it and Charles Chaffee standing on the curb to the right of the little boy. The man in the driver's seat is thought to be Sattuck's brother, L. B. Fiske, a Shattuck employee, also shared the driving in this event.

Chapter 4 - The Ohio Automobile Company

The rains came upon leaving Albany, the third day of the run. With the rain came steering and traction difficulties. Most cars rode on tires without treads. Wrapping rope around the rear wheels proved fruitless. Hatcher, coasting down a steep hill, turned too sharply and the resulting skid pulled the rear tires off the rims. The other Packards arrived within the allotted time. Hatcher was able to make the necessary repairs, although he arrived late. The Packard team was wet but still intact.

Others were not so lucky and some had just had enough. John Jacob Astor, tired of fighting the cold and rain, turned his Gasmobile over to his chauffeur and went home. Some contestants had most of the spare parts they needed following them in other conveyances. Others waited at Railway Express offices for needed items and worked through the night to repair ailing vehicles.

Day four of the event, from Herkimer to Syracuse, continued in the rain and fifty-five competitors were still on the road. The noon stop at Oneida was shortened to a half-hour to allow a run straight through to Syracuse, where night control was opened at 1:30 in the afternoon. Nobody made it by that time. The roads had turned into a morass, and there was no thought of racing. Nevertheless, all five Packards made it through Control in the allotted time, the last being Satterfield who suffered a broken axle, repaired it en route, and arrived at 7:53 p.m. The field was now down to forty-eight contestants.

The following day's run to Rochester was eighty-seven miles, and weather continued to disintegrate. Only thirty-nine cars made it to the control point on time that evening. James Ward's Packard with Weiss aboard was now in second place, behind Bishop's Panhard. Only McMurtry's Packard experienced difficulty that day, but he did arrive within the allotted time.

The last day's run was to be from Rochester to Buffalo, with an appropriate finale planned at the Pan American Exposition – but fate intervened. While the contestants were slogging their way through the mud to Rochester on Thursday, September 12th, President McKinley died. He had been shot by a deranged anarchist, at a reception at the Exposition eight days before. The organizers of the run met the following morning and decided to end the event at Rochester. The three Packards

Packards

Are built for combined *reliability* and *speed* over any roads. Ask the man who owns one. Our machines can and do *prove their efficiency* in every detail. Descriptive catalogue free.

We shall exhibit at the New York show.

OHIO AUTOMOBILE CO.

Warren, - - - - **Ohio**

The first advertisement using the slogan "Ask the man who owns one" as it appeared in Motor Age, October 31, 1901, prior to the second New York Auto Show.

entered by the company were shipped back to Warren immediately and the tired drivers followed. William Doud wrote in his log: "Ward and Hatcher home tonight. We probably won highest American honors". He was right. The highest average speed, from start to finish, was maintained by the Bishop Panhard, next came James Ward and then Hatcher. The Apperson brothers' cars were in fourth and fifth place. Four Packards received a first class certificate for averaging twelve to fifteen miles per hour. Satterfield, in spite of his broken axle, received a second class certificate for ten to twelve miles per hour average. Only half of the vehicles that started the contest finished it – but every one of the Packards achieved that goal. It was a record about which the company could, and did, boast.

After the spectacular performance of the Packard automobiles during the New York to Buffalo event the Ohio Automobile Co. began a more active advertising campaign, based not only on reliability but also on its growing reputation. The name Packard was now frequently referred to in automotive circles, and the owners felt prospective buyers should know more about the company. As the time for the Second Automobile Show approached, the company ran an ad in the October 31, 1901, edition of *Motor Age* using the soon-to-be famous, Packard slogan, "Ask the Man Who Owns One", for the first time. This short, straightforward ad paraphrased words George Weiss had used in his statements to the press many times before, and added this new phrase which would outlive all previous pronouncements and become a staple of Packard ads for years to come. The ad read:

PACKARDS

Are built for combined "reliability" and "speed" over any roads. Ask the man who owns one. Our machines can, and do, "prove their efficiency" in every detail. Descriptive catalogue free. We shall exhibit at the New York Show.

The origin of this famous slogan has become the stuff of legend. One of the most popular scenarios has James Ward's secretary entering his office with a letter from a Pittsburg man desiring information about the Packard car. "What shall I tell him?" the secretary asks. To which Packard replies "Tell him I'll be over to talk with him – no, wait, just tell

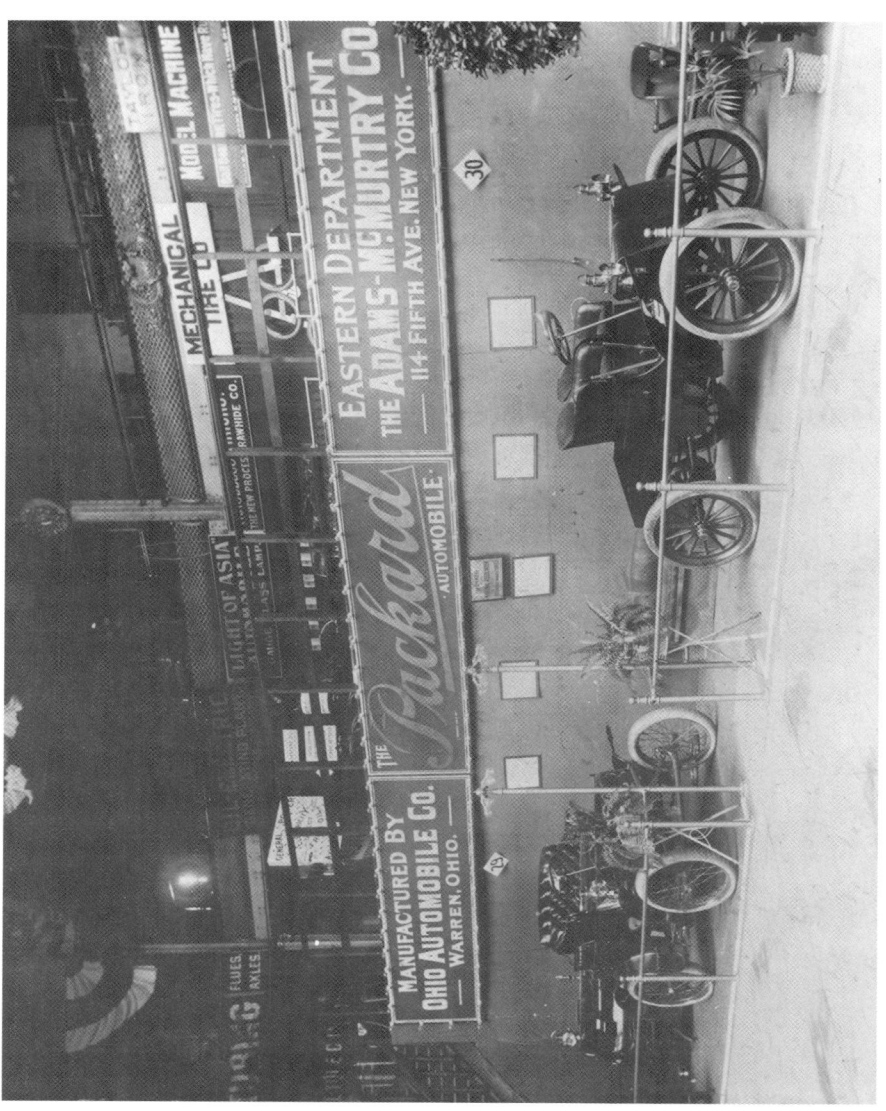

The Packard Exhibit at the second New York Auto Show, Madison Square Garden, November 2-9, 1901, was organized by George Weiss. He displayed a Model C and a Model F prototype (space #30) built on a Model C chassis which lacked the front radiator that later became its most recognizable feature.

Chapter 4 - The Ohio Automobile Company

The Model F Special at Washington Square in New York City prior to being displayed at the Second Annual Auto Show in space #30. This side view shows the shorter Model C wheelbase which was used in this prototype.

The Model F Special at Washington Square, New York City, prior to being displayed at the second Auto Show (space #30). This was an experimental prototype built on a Model C chassis and lacks the front radiator found on later production models.

Chapter 4 - The Ohio Automobile Company

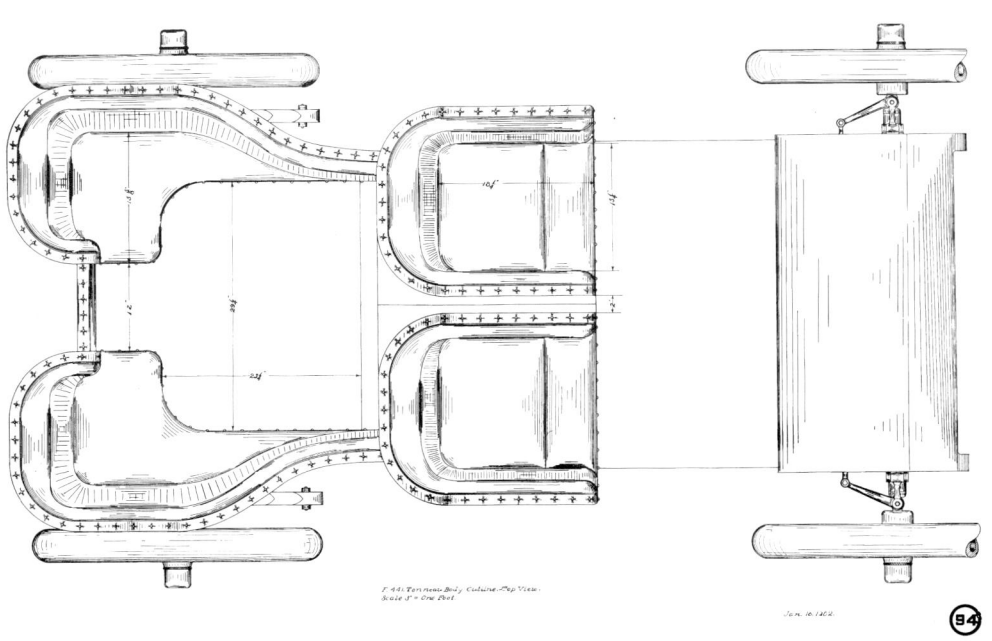

The six-passenger experimental Model C with rear bench seats facing each other and a radiator mounted in the front. This unusual automobile may have been the test vehicle for the radiator destined for the new 1902 Model F.

An updated feature drawing, January 16, 1902, of a removable rear entry tonneau body style used on the Model F.

Two views of the Model C Special with Bert Hatcher and Olive Packard in the front seat and four office girls in the rear tonneau.

him to ask the man who owns one". Whatever the origin, these words would from that day forward be linked to the Packard automobile.

The last big event for the Ohio Automobile Co. in 1901 was the Second National Auto Show at Madison Square Garden. On September 16, 1901, William Doud had noted in his diary that the new Model F had been completed and was running "beautifully". The major change was the addition of a third gear between low and high, as well as a change to a sliding gear system from the previous two-speed planetary. The body was to be hung low on a drop frame, constructed without the underframe used on previous models. The most noticeable change to come was the repositioning of the radiator from underneath the chassis to the front where it was very much in view. Other changes were larger (34"x4") tires, and the decision to make red the standard body color.

The company was very anxious to make an impressive showing at Madison Square Garden but there were major problems. Production was hindered due to a seven week strike by machinists, during the two months previous to the event, which made it impossible for the company to display the new Model F in its intended form. On October 30th William Doud noted that two "new" Model Fs had been shipped to New York. One of these cars was displayed along with a still-available Model C. There are several photos of the "new" Model F that in all probability was the September prototype because although it had many Model F features it was built on a Model C chassis and lacked the distinctive front radiator, the most prominent feature of the Model Fs that followed.

There was talk at the show concerning the optimum number of cylinders a car should have. Ward was convinced his single cylinder engine was the right one for his particular vehicle, and that his vehicle was the right car for the American roads of the time. He defended his position by saying: "In the past year we have seen no valid reasons for abandoning our general system.... The objections to the single cylinder we frankly acknowledge, but these apply to machines constructed on the old lines entirely. By our system of spring drive and automatic firing control their objections are, we believe, entirely overcome. We have, of course, heard the popular clamor for multiple cylinder engines placed upright in front of the carriage so as to be readily accessible. We acknowledge the necessity of easy accessibility with these multiple cylinder machines, but we state positively that our own engine, and all its [parts] are as readily accessible as in any other type. We also positively

Model C assembly floor, 1901.

Chapter 4 - The Ohio Automobile Company

affirm that it is unnecessary to get at the parts for constant tinkering. There is a decided advantage, too, in the underhung engine with flywheel and main weight near the center of the car, in improved stability and the proper distribution of weight. This distribution of weight is with more than half of the weight on the rear wheels, giving the greatest possible freedom from skidding and maximum traction which is noticeably lacking at times in those machines having the engines up front."

During the show a reporter asked George Weiss about total Packard production to that date and his reply was 165. It is possible he was going by motor numbers (that would be the actual count plus twenty) and adding units in process at the plant. However, using the information gleaned from William Doud's "Packard & Weiss" ledger, and James Ward's letters to G.L., it would seem to be in error. It is not known when the last C was completed, but according to a personal notebook of Ward Packard the total number was 82. At the time of the New York show all eyes were turning toward the new Model F, but as of October only two had been built. Not counting the Model Fs, final production figures for all previous Packard models (assuming the last C had been built—which undoubtedly had not happened) only totaled 117 units, distributed as follows:

Model A	5
Model B	29
Model C	82
Model E	1
	117

The Model C production information was transcribed from a James Ward Packard notebook by Duane L. Bohnstedt, a Packard employee, in 1956. Mr. Bohnstedt had a great interest in the company history as well as access to the company files that he often studied during his free time. He provided the author with a copy of Ward's notes relating to unit numbers 55 through 140 including all Model Cs, the E and three Fs. The full text of this document is found in Appendix C.

In spite of problems caused by the strike the Packard presence at the Garden was a resounding success. George Weiss was again in charge of the company exhibit. James Ward arrived the second day. Packards were selling well off the floor and the response was so enthusiastic that bigger headquarters were decided upon for the New

The 1902 Model F that was produced in the spring of that year.

York show room. On December 11th Adams-McMurtry moved to 317 West 59th Street where they invested heavily in a larger showroom and more complete service department.

One of the features of this new facility was the repair shop described in the June 21st issue of *"The Automobile"*. It stated that it was "not merely a place for ordinary repair which necessitates little machine work, but is fully equipped for any and all jobs which may be needed". According to the article, unfinished forgings were kept in stock and machined as needed. The shop had its own gasoline powered generator, two engine lathes, a universal milling machine, a shaper, drill press and even a forge. It also had a hoist which was capable of lifting the vehicle high enough to permit a workman "to stand upright under it". This was certainly an impressive facility for 1901. It seems as if it had the capability of building a Packard almost from scratch.

It had been a busy two years for the company. The cars had been a phenomenal success, a good dealer network had been established, and the company could now boast that there were Packard owners from coast to coast. However, the problem still existed to find the money not only to sustain production but to finance the necessary expansion. 1902 would be another year of radical change.

Henry Bourne Joy

Chapter 5
Henry Bourne Joy
and the Detroit Investors

At the time of the second New York Automobile Show Henry Bourne Joy, a prominent Detroit businessman, joined the ranks of Packard owners. He had been intrigued with horseless carriages since 1898 when he saw the machines being built by Henry Ford and had an interest in buying one. Mr. Ford advised Joy to wait since they were in a stage of development and said the newer models would be better. At that time Ford was experiencing financial difficulties and heeding his advice, Joy put off buying a motor vehicle.

Henry Joy was a member of a wealthy Detroit family. His father had made a fortune with the Michigan Central, and the Burlington and Quincy railroads which later became the Burlington Northern Railroad. He was educated at the Phillips Academy in Andover, Massachusetts, and at the Sheffield Scientific Institute at Yale University. Joy was a man with a commanding personality and a focused mind.

In 1886 he began his business career in family-controlled enterprises, first as a clerk in the Peninsular (railroad) Car Company of Detroit where he soon became paymaster and then assistant treasurer. In November 1890 he became secretary of the Fort Street Union Depot, and a year later he took over the treasury duties as well. By 1900, Joy had become its president.

Henry Ford's advice, to wait, didn't curb Joy's interest in the horseless carriage. He looked at many vehicles being manufactured at that time. Especially in New York, where most manufacturers had representatives and where he often went for business reasons. Joy and his brother-in-law, Truman Newberry were in New York, perusing the automobile show rooms just before the opening of the second Auto Show in 1901. Joy, being a railroad man, had a predilection for steam carriages, since they had a reputation for being easy to start – a constant problem for most internal combustion engines. However, on a previous occasion he and Newberry had been inspecting a steam carriage when the sight glass, a tube which indicates the level of water in the boiler,

The Ohio Automobile Co. in 1901. The house in the foreground was built for the office and drafting personnel

burst in Newberry's face. That episode seemed to dampen Joy's interest in steam for the propulsion of road vehicles.

During their rounds of the showrooms, possibly the same day, Joy and Newberry visited the Adams-McMurtry agency where they saw two Packards parked in front on the street. Joy, who had heard about Packards, asked the drivers if they were easy to start and received an affirmative answer. At that point, it is said, a team pulling a fire engine came clanging down the street and the two drivers ran to their vehicles, switched on the ignition, gave the cranks a couple of turns, and then sped off in pursuit. Both Joy and Newberry were so impressed that they decided then and there to become Packard owners.

Joy and Newberry attended the second Auto Show which was held November 2nd through the 9th, 1901, and when they returned to Detroit Joy told the press he was taking delivery of a year-old model and ordering a new 1902 Model F for future delivery. He also stated that the Packard, in his opinion, was "one of the best in the country", and that he had purchased 100 shares of Ohio Automobile Company stock.

The automobile Joy bought was actually a Model C with tiller steering, an option offered on the early Model Cs. Nevertheless, he was obviously satisfied with the vehicle and he was photographed in it along with Mrs. Joy as late as 1907. The caption, along with the photo in the *Detroit Free Press*, states that this was Joy's first automobile.

On January 23, 1902, Joy bought another 150 shares of Ohio Automobile stock and showed up at the stockholders' meeting that was held the following day. He now owned $25,000.00 worth of stock in the company and it was obvious he had more than a passing interest in the Packard venture.

Even before the stockholders meeting he had contacted George Weiss, who he had met at the Auto Show, relative to the purchase of a Baker Electric for Mrs. Joy. At that time, when most men were fascinated with gasoline vehicles, very few women shared their enthusiasm. They opted for the simple, quiet, and easy to operate electric conveyances. Mrs. Weiss had a Baker Stanhope, and that is probably the reason George Weiss became involved in the Joy purchase.

The new 12,000 square foot building for automotive assembly completed in January 1902.

Chapter 5 - Henry Bourne Joy and the Detriot Investors

Henry Joy's interest in the company and its progress continued after the January meeting, and he made several trips to Warren during the spring and summer of 1902. Although his name was mentioned in Ward's diary many times, it was October before it appeared in the company minutes. During this period, however, he and Ward must have had many discussions about future development, as Joy toyed with the idea of becoming more deeply involved in what he considered to be a very promising business.

The Ohio Automobile Company was growing by leaps and bounds in the spring of 1902. A new 12,000 square foot two story frame structure had just been completed at the time of the January board meeting, the third building to be dedicated to automotive operations. Having overcome the delays caused by the strike prior to the second Automobile Show, the Model F was in full production and sales were keeping pace with the growth of the physical plant—in spite of the fact that the Model F had a price tag of $2,500.00—double that of the Model A. All of this activity must have made a favorable impression on Henry Joy.

Both the price and the size of the Packard automobile had increased substantially since the first models were sold in the spring of 1900. The Model A had a 71 inch wheelbase and sold for $1,250.00. It was followed by the Model B with a 76 inch wheelbase and a price of $1,750.00. The Model C carried a price of $1,750.00 but it had a larger engine (12 hp) on a 75 inch wheelbase which provided a better weight to horsepower ratio and, consequently, better performance. Although the Model F used the same basic engine as the Model C it was the largest Packard to date and depended on other features to justify its $2,500.00 price tag.

The major distinguishing features of the Model F were the larger front fenders and a wider hood to accommodate the front radiator which had not appeared on the prototype at the New York Auto Show. The emphasis now was on the variety of body styles made possible with the longer wheelbase. The removable rear tonneau was one of those features. It could be entered through a rear door when the center rear seat cushion was raised to allow access. This made it possible to carry several passengers with some degree of comfort, as was illustrated in their advertising. Without the tonneau in place it became a roadster.

1902 Model F's on the production floor.

Chapter 5 - Henry Bourne Joy and the Detroit Investors

The Model F was built in a series of specialty shops. After the chassis was fabricated, it was placed in a primary assembly shop where the wheels, engine, fuel and water tanks, oiling system and other miscellaneous parts were added to make it an operative unit. Then smooth, all-white, Goodrich tires were mounted and engine tests were performed. At this point the completed chassis was rolled to the next building to be mated to the desired body style. Before final assembly both the body and chassis were sent to the paint shop where they were brush painted separately, before being bolted together. The wiring department was next where one man worked a half-day assembling and mounting the harness. When completed, the car was taken out on North Avenue for a test run to be sure everything was in working order. The test mechanic was responsible for making any adjustments required before the machine was pronounced ready for delivery.

On March 14th Henry Joy's new Model F arrived in Detroit, and that city's *"Journal"* announced the event with a headline, "It's a Blue Devil". The paper went on to say, "It is a gasoline road machine with a blue body, red wheels and plenty of brass work, giving the machine an elegant appearance. Mr. Joy secured it this week from Warren, Ohio, having sold his runabout to F.B. Stearns. The only other [Packard] in Detroit is the Red Devil, owned by Truman H. Newberry. Mr. Joy says his Blue Devil is not intended for racing and has a maximum speed of 25 miles per hour. It is a two seated affair and one of the most expensive automobiles in Detroit". Actually, there was a third Packard in the city at that time. A Model C had been sold to a Miss Fletcher there in early 1902.

By April, Joy was beginning to influence the affairs of the Ohio Automobile Company. On one of his first visits to New York Ward noted in his diary that he had met with Joy and Charles Schmidt on April 6th, at Bronx Park, to examine a 15 hp two cylinder Mors. A few days later on April 12th, Ward, Weiss, Joy, and Schmidt had breakfast together in Warren. The future of the company was discussed, and it was decided to hire Schmidt at four dollars a day. He started work four days later.

Charles Schmidt, a Frenchman with over eight years' experience designing cars for firms in Europe, had recently been with the Mors factory as plant superintendent and part-time race driver. He had attracted Joy's attention for work he had done on the Mors chassis. The

The 1903 body shop with F units on the floor.

Chapter 5 - Henry Bourne Joy and the Detroit Investors

contemporary Mors was powered by a flat twin cylinder engine with a displacement of 850 cc—so it would seem Schmidt was not wedded to Ward's philosophy regarding single cylinder engines.

Schmidt was a man with considerable ability in both the design and production areas, plus he was an able problem solver —- a trait that would be needed as new models were developed. After only eighteen days in Warren, Schmidt was given full charge of the plant production facilities as well as some engineering and design duties. His presence would influence the development of new multi-cylinder engines which Henry Joy seemed to favor. Although Joy was not in a position at this time to dictate company policy his ideas and suggestions were definitely being taken into consideration with the tacit approval of the Packard brothers and George Weiss.

Ward Packard, like other engineers to this day, was taught that "the simplest solution to a problem is the best solution". This approach to design was certainly uppermost in his mind when he first realized the French and other Europeans were building multi-cylinder automobiles. More cylinders – more problems! He made his stance on this issue very clear, up to and through 1902. Ward was once quoted by a reporter as saying that "more than one cylinder on a Packard would be like two tails on a cat— you just don't need it." Ward sincerely believed this, and made every effort to bring any doubters around to his way of thinking. The company even went so far as to publish an amusing little booklet entitled:

"Six to one, or Wasted Pride, Perspiration and Profanity".

"Now I want it clearly understood that I'm patriotic, ride American machines, with 'PACKARD'S' Yankee Doodle Single Cylinder. For American roads 'PACKARD' automobiles have no peers. When I see a French machine go gliding by and a friend says: 'Oh, isn't that fine'. I can't help but think – six – six – what a mix. Really you observe I'm a trifle prejudiced. France – glorious France. France for paintings, sculptures and vin ordinaire, don't you know, - but that's 'bout all.

"Before entering upon an automobile existence, look around you. Get a machine that will stand the wear and tear, the bumping and thumping. Get one, not so complicated, but [one] you can understand without a polytechnical course. Get one as

The 1902 Model G Special sold to William Rockefeller. This was the company's first multi-cylinder car. It had a horizontally opposed two cylinder engine rated at 24 hp.

good as the 'PACKARD' and you will get all that's coming to you. 'Ask the man who owns one'"

Nevertheless, even after making statements of this kind, Ward must have begun to realize that as the Packard automobiles became larger and heavier they were going to need more power, and the only practical way to generate that power was to increase the number of cylinders. Both Ward and Hatcher had reached this decision by the spring of 1902 some time before Schmidt was hired, because Ward recorded in his diary that the first two cylinder Packard, the Model G, was completed on June 29th. Three days later Joy was in Warren to see it. He certainly must have been aware that a two cylinder vehicle was being designed when he introduced Schmidt to Ward Packard and they examined the two cylinder Mors on April 6th.

The Model G was the largest and the heaviest Packard yet, and required all the power of the 24 hp opposed cylinder engine designed for it. With a wheelbase of 91 inches and 36 inch wheels supported by ball bearings encased in huge bronze hubs, it tipped the scales at almost 4000 lbs. The frame was made of channel steel and rested on semi-elliptic front springs with full elliptics in the rear.

It was the Model G engine which drew the most attention. It was described in *The Horseless Age* as "a horizontal opposed double cylinder [engine] of 24 horsepower, located under the body. The crankshaft is parallel with the axles, the cylinders are located on the left side of the center line of the vehicle and the flywheel is located on the right hand side—each cylinder of the engine has a separate carburetor, and the timing of the spark is done by a centrifugal governor, which revolves with the cam shaft and shifts the two ignition cams—the ignition is by jump spark. A three cell storage battery in the front boot furnishes the current to the igniters. There are two water tanks under the main seats, which hold approximately four gallons each. One of the gasoline tanks is located under the boot and the other below the body at the extreme rear." These tanks were connected by a tube with a shut-off valve.

The Model G fenders were made of aluminum and the front seats were attached separately to conform to the buyer's wishes. All seats were upholstered in tufted leather, and "to afford the passengers additional comfort the footboards are inclined". *The Horseless Age* went

A front view of the Model G showing the huge bronze hubs required to support its 4,000 lb. weight.

on to say the Model G could carry eight persons if the tonneau was substituted for the rear seat option. And this load would apparently not tax the brakes too badly as there was a new double acting brake on the "secondary change speed shaft and a foot operated brake on the differential drum".

There were very few Model G's produced, probably only 4, but the engine proved to be reliable. William Rockefeller bought the first one, even before the model was announced. *The Automobile and Motor Review*, however, called the car "ponderous—a true leviathan—without any apparent advantage to be gained by its enormous weight". It did not sell well.

Meanwhile, Model F's were selling as fast as they could be produced, and even the older single cylinder Packards were making a name for the Ohio Automobile Company on several fronts. On April 26th, the Long Island Auto Club sponsored their second contest on a route from Jamaica to Oyster Bay and return. Alden McMurtry represented the Ohio Automobile Company along with Fred C. March from Warren in a second Packard, and both were among the twenty one finishers awarded blue ribbons for completing the 100-mile course without a stop.

On August 2nd Packard owner H.E. Clapp of Attleboro, Massachusetts, drove his Model C to the top of Mount Washington, New Hampshire, and it became not only the heaviest vehicle to reach the summit but also the first car powered with a gasoline engine. Clapp had read about the feats of F.O. Stanley and others making the ascent in steamers and decided it was time to prove that anything a steam vehicle could do, a Packard with a gasoline engine could do better. To stress the point he took a Mr. R.C. Reed along as a passenger!

Another memorable run, the longest ever to date, was made by Chicago businessman, E.B. Martin, who drove his Model F from that city to New York starting on August 9th, and reaching his destination on August 22nd. Upon his arrival he was interviewed by a reporter from *The Horseless Age* who commented "evidence of severe usage was plain – tires were pitted and cracked – but after being worked on by Adams & McMurtry the machine bore no sign of deterioration". Quite a testimonial!

As demand for the very popular F increased, the need to expand the physical plant became evident, and on July 2nd the construction of

The drafting room, 1902.

the fourth and last factory building to be built in Warren was announced. It was to be a 32,000 square foot two story brick structure located just east of the existing facilities, which would have the capacity to double factory output —- but it would not be completed until January 1903*.

During the early years almost every component of the Packard automobile was manufactured at the Warren factory. The Packard brothers found it difficult, if not impossible, to buy items of the quality they insisted upon. Mr. Walter Hackett, who had been William Doud Packard's secretary during the late twenties, wrote an article for *MOTOR* magazine in 1931 in which he mentioned the Packards' problems with materials. W.D. had often spoken to Hackett about the troubles they had experienced during the Warren years. He said, they were "almost always related to materials rather than design. There were continual breakages". The company soon began making many parts and sub-assemblies because many suppliers used poor materials, and they could not get the quality they demanded. On several occasions they received so many defective parts that it interrupted production. Once, they turned down so many wheel assemblies that the supplier refused to make any more. Bearings and gears were a special problem. In many cases they had to use steel that the Navy had developed for armor-piercing shells. They also used shell steel for gear blanks because most steel available from domestic sources was not good enough for their needs. Some early cylinder castings were also a problem and they had to be imported from France.

In another instance Hackett relates the problem "involved both design and materials [and] came when we put a governor on our spark. We were afraid to let the engine run too fast and so [we] had the spark stopped at what we thought was a safe speed. One of our owners learned that he could [readjust] the governor [to let it run at a higher speed] and after he did so, ran circles around everybody in town for some time. Finally he [went] a little too fast and the flywheel flew off, making a nasty wreck".

---

*This building was still standing in 1965. It served as a warehouse for the Ohio Lamp Plant of General Electric. They bought it, along with the lamp business, from the Packard brothers in 1910. When G.E. decided to raze the facility that year some employees found tools bearing the name of the Ohio Automobile Company which are now displayed in the National Packard Museum.

Two photos of George L. Weiss in the driver's seat of a Model F during the 500 mile New York to Boston Time Trial in October 1902. The passengers have not been identified, but it is known that Mr. R.P. Scott accompanied Weiss as an observer.

Chapter 5 - Henry Bourne Joy and the Detriot Investors

In early October the Automobile Club of America sponsored an event they called the New York to Boston Time Trial. The round trip was to take six days and covered a distance of 500 miles through Norwalk, New Haven, Hartford, Springfield, and Worcester. It was a different type of event from earlier endurance runs and it required the contestants to maintain 14 mph average for each of the six days. It tested the drivers even more than the cars. Any car which averaged over or under the designated 14 mph lost points relative to the amount of variation noted at each observation post. George Weiss remarked after the run, "It takes a man who knows his machine exceedingly well [to maintain the average speed]. The inclination is to let the car out a little on good level stretches, but if you do, you make it still harder for yourself to keep within the time limits on the rest of the way to the control [point]. Running in high gear, as a good driver is naturally inclined to do whenever he can, there are times when the motor is barely turning over, and [by] throwing in the lower gears you take more chances of ignition and other motor troubles. My driver frequently warned me that the motor would be liable to balk, and cause a penalized stop if I persisted, as I did, in picking my way up some steep hills [in] the high gear, relying on working the clutch, for keeping both the motor and the car going. When [this] is kept up for six hours the mental strain is something enormous". (It would seem as if they didn't worry about wear on the clutch in those contests.)

Sixty-eight of the seventy-five cars that started completed the course, and the Ohio Automobile Company was well represented. Weiss drove a Model F loaned from Adams-McMurtry, as did Fred C. March. Henry Joy drove his personal Model F, the Blue Devil, providing the Detroit papers with news of the event and at the same time coaxing Goodrich to advertise the fact that the Packards used their tires. Boston Packard dealer H.B. Shattuck & Son entered a fourth car driven by their Ben Smith. Last, but not least, Harlan W. Whipple entered the fifth Packard, his Model G, which had been much maligned in *The Automobile and Motor Review* for its "ponderous" weight. Whipple was about to prove the Model G critics wrong.

George Weiss defended both Whipple and the Ohio Automobile Company in a statement to the press saying, "Few persons have any idea what it means for a manufacturer to enter a machine, very much heavier that anything previously built, in a contest of this kind, but people

The gold medal George L. Weiss received for his performance in a Model F during the New York to Boston Time Trial. Harlan W. Whipple won a similar medal in his Model G.

don't look into those things deeply. They like to [criticize] anything they have not seen before.

"There are certain vital points in automobile construction where you cannot afford to take chances, and the steering knuckle is one of them. Besides, when you put wheels under as heavy a car as this one is, on ball bearings, you must protect those bearings. Now, on this car it was particularly desirable to have the steering pivots as close up against the hub as possible, nearly in line with the plane of the spokes. In order to [accomplish] this, it was necessary to reduce the [bearing surface on the inside of the hub] and correspondingly increase it on the outside of the hub. [Without this extended hub], the ball bearing surface would have been insufficient". Nevertheless, *The Horseless Age* wondered about the "stupendous destruction which would take place if two of the vehicles should try to pass on a narrow country road and accidentally 'lock horns'."

In spite of the adverse attention it was a good day for the Packards. Harlan Whipple had the best score, and won one of the only two medals awarded at the conclusion of the Trial. George Weiss won the other medal with the Model F.

A special stockholders' meeting was scheduled for October 13, 1902, immediately after the New York to Boston Time Trial, which proved to be one of the most significant in the history of the company. 1,500 shares were represented at the meeting, either by the owners in person or by proxy. The founders held 1,174 shares. Weiss was not present but he was represented by proxy. This was to be last board meeting in which the founders would still have the votes to control the destiny of the company.

At the meeting, it was resolved to change the name from the Ohio Automobile Company to the Packard Motor Car Company. William Doud Packard offered the motion and it was carried unanimously. It was further resolved to elect a new board of eight directors at the next annual stockholders' meeting to be held on January 29, 1903. Also approved, by the stockholders the same day was a previously agreed upon decision to increase the capital stock, once again, to 5,000 shares, authorizing 2,500 additional shares for sale. Joy, his family, friends and associates would be the buyers. With the consummation of these sales the future of the Packard Motor Car Company would be in the hands of Henry B. Joy.

Unfortunately, very little is known about the events which led up to the decisions made on October 13th, but there is no doubt that everything had been worked out in advance before they sat down at the table. There was no evidence of any opposition to the resolutions approved at the proceedings. Although Henry Joy's name doesn't appear anywhere in the minutes of the meeting, his influence certainly played the major role in setting the agenda. Everyone present seemed to know that the Ohio Automobile Company could not continue its rapid rate of growth without an infusion of capital. It was also clear that the founders could not raise the necessary funds without selling assets. Both the Packard brothers and George Weiss had substantial assets available. The Packards had the New York & Ohio Company and Packard Electric, and Weiss possessed a strong portfolio of valuable securities, but none of the founders seemed willing to dispose of their holdings to fund the automobile venture. It was also painfully evident that even by pooling their assets they could not match the financial backing that Joy and his associates could bring to bear.

From the time Joy convinced Ward to hire Schmidt, he was making an obvious effort to introduce Ward to his Detroit associates. Ward had already met Truman Newberry, Joy's brother-in-law, another enthusiastic Packard owner, and he knew that Joy's wife, the former Helen Hall Newberry, was the daughter of John Newberry, one of Detroit's most prominent citizens. On April 20, 1902, according to Ward's dairy, he visited the prestigious Grosse Pointe Country Club with Joy and Russell A. Alger, another wealthy Detroit businessman who would later become a significant stockholder in the Packard Motor Car Company.

During the spring Ward made several visits with Joy to Detroit and must have realized the extent of Joy's influence in the financial community of that city. It is certain there were discussions concerning the future of the company, and Joy must have expressed his ideas relating to the part he would like to play in financing future growth. Everything depended upon whether or not the partners were willing to allow Joy to take a larger stake in the company. He was obviously prepared to do so, and he certainly demonstrated there was a strong group of investors ready to join him.

Chapter 5 - Henry Bourne Joy and the Detriot Investors

Meanwhile, William Doud, who normally handled the finances of the Packard enterprises, was struggling with their monetary dilemma. While he was in Chicago promoting the New York & Ohio lamps, he noted in his diary that he had had supper with his cousin Levi, a banker, and they had discussed borrowing money. The Packards normally financed their business expansion out of current revenues. In general they were averse to borrowing to any great extent. Levi, however, didn't see any problem with it as long as it was based on tangible assets. Increasing capital by selling more stock was also discussed and his cousin intimated that if he cared to sell more shares in the auto company "he would probably like to take some".

Many things were going on at this time which required the Packard brothers to make some basic decisions as to the type of business they would pursue in future years. Two days after his return from Chicago, W.D. and Ward met with F.S. Terry of the National Electric Lamp Company to discuss the possible sale of the New York & Ohio Company to his firm. Their reason for discussing such a sale is not known. Was the money to be used to expand the automotive operation or for some other purpose? It is known that the Packard brothers were trying to buy two other electric companies about the same time. It is also known that W.D. had discussed selling the automobile business earlier in the summer, an option that his brother probably did not look upon with favor.

According to *The Horseless Age*, Mr. H.B. Wick of Youngstown made an offer to buy a half interest in the Ohio Automobile Company on September 29, 1902, but they did not give any dollar amount relating to the offer. W.D. notes in his diary "$50,000 now, balance later". What the balance was is not known, but the offer was not accepted.

Henry Joy's Detroit associates were quick to join him after the decisions of October 13th were finalized. Russell Alger, Jr. was the first to come aboard with an investment of $50,000, and he was followed by Fred M. Alger with another $25,000. Joy added $25,000 to his previous purchases, bringing his total investment to $50,000, and his brother Richard P. Joy joined him with $10,000 more. The Newberrys, Truman H. and John S. both came in with $25,000 each. Other investors among the original group were: Phillip H. McMillan, $50,000; Joseph Boyer, $25,000; C.A. DuCharme, $10,000 and D.M. Ferry, Jr. $5,000. These purchases represented all of the additional shares authorized on October 13th.

DETROIT MEN BUY AUTO WORKS

BIG OHIO FACTORY TO BE MOVED HERE WHEN SITE IS OBTAINED.

Russell A. Alger, Jr. and D. M Ferry, Jr., in the Company Organized With $500,000 Capital.

One of the most important automobile works in the United States, at Warren, O., known as the Ohio Automobile works, has been acquired by a new company made up mostly of young business men of Detroit. This company, with a capital of $500,000, all paid in, was organized last week. The works will be operated in Warren, O., until a site can be obtained in Detroit, when the works will be moved here and operations begun on a much larger scale. It is said that with the new capital the output will be increased tenfold.

The Detroit men are Russell A. Alger, Jr., Fred M. Alger, John S. and Truman Newberry, H. B. and R. P. Joy, Charles A. Ducharme, D. M. Ferry, Jr., William O. and Philip H. McMillan and Joseph Boyer.

The two Packards who have been the main men in the concern heretofore will remain in the enterprise, and the company will bear their name. The board of directors consists of Truman Newberry, Harry B. Joy, a Mr. Weiss of Cleveland, the two Packards, Phillip H. McMillan, Joseph Boyer and R. A. Alger, Jr. The other officers have not yet been elected but the new company is now in control.

Detriot Free Press, October 1902

Chapter 5 - Henry Bourne Joy and the Detriot Investors

Each investor paid one half of his total subscription in cash at the time of purchase; a total of $125,000 which was immediately available to meet current expenses. These shares had a par value of $250,000 and when Joy's original investments of $25,000 was added, the Detroit investors controlled $275,000 of Packard Motor Car Company stock. *The Detroit Free Press* noted the sale of the Company.

It is not known exactly how much money the Packard brothers and George L. Weiss had invested in their automotive venture at the time the Detroit group entered the picture, but it was clear they no longer had control. At the October 13th meeting the founders only held 1174 shares of stock with a par value of $117,400 and they could have possibly depended on the votes of another 326 shares ($32,600) held by friends and family members, a total of 1500 shares ($150,000)*.

At the October stockholders' meeting, when the name was changed to the Packard Motor Car Company there was no mention of any move to Detroit, but without a doubt such a move was a fait accompli. The name change was made to facilitate such a move. Henry Joy had certainly told his associates of his plans for such a move, and the Warren plant was obviously inadequate for the plans Joy envisioned. A new factory had to be built. Joy and his colleagues were not going to build it in Warren when all of their interests were in Detroit.

The day following the decisive meetings, a reporter from the *Warren Tribune* asked James Ward if a move to Detroit was anticipated and he replied, "There were no such plans. The subject was, in fact, not even brought up among the stockholders, and it is not likely that a large and already well equipped plant will be dismantled and another built." The *Tribune* also noted that the motorcar would still be called the Packard, and that soon the present output of one car a day would be increased to ten times that.

These remarks temporarily encouraged the local workforce. It was true a new building was nearing completion which would allow a higher rate of production in 1903, but it wasn't going to last. The insiders knew this. George Weiss resented the way the Detroit investors were

* Numbers taken from the minutes of the October 13, 1902, stockholders' meeting, Warren, Ohio.

Model F chassis assembly in Warren, early 1903.

Chapter 5 - Henry Bourne Joy and the Detriot Investors

taking over and did not see eye to eye with Joy. On November 15, 1902, Weiss tendered his resignation as a director and vice president of the Packard Motor Car Company. James Ward tried to convince Joy to keep Weiss on as part of the business. Joy wrote back to Ward and said "We think it would be wise for the company not to take on again any business relations with Mr. Weiss. Mr. Weiss has severed his business relations with the Packard Motor Car Company and we think, if it meets with your approval, that it is best that no more trouble should be incurred through renewing business relationships". The "with your approval" thinly veiled who was now in charge. He continued, "I do not like to feel that your letter of December 27 advises the appointment of Mr. Weiss because I feel that you ought to be able to get along to a better advantage without him —he may sell [his stock] to anyone to whom he pleases. We are doing our level best to—make that stock valuable to him. I think we should succeed".

A few days later W.D. ran into Weiss on the Cleveland train and recorded that Weiss was "very much disgruntled with the policy of the Motor Car Company". In March Weiss inquired if the company would exchange machines for his capital stock, but Joy said it would be "impractical for this company to exchange from a legal point of view". James Ward Packard recorded in his diary on March 30, 1905, over a year after he also had given up an active role in the company, that George L. Weiss had severed all connections with the company he had helped start. G.L. traded his 300 shares for twelve leftover 1904 Model Ls which he sold from his home in Cleveland. As the years went by and Packard prospered he certainly had cause to regret his decision.

Next to the birthday of the Packard automobile that is considered to be July 3, 1899, the day Hatcher agreed to join "Packard & Weiss", October 13, 1902, must be considered to be the second milestone in the history of the company. With Henry B. Joy at the helm and its immediate future secured, it was ready to move onto a larger stage. Under the Packards and Weiss, the company had manufactured fine cars on a small scale and built a nationwide reputation for quality. It is not known if the Packard Automobile Company could have continued to thrive had it remained in Warren, but for now the future was in Detroit—and the move would not be easy.

The Detriot Packard Plant under construction, summer 1903.

Chapter 6

The Move to Detroit

In spite of Ward's words to the contrary, it was impossible to keep word of the move to Detroit a secret. Everyone knew that Joy and all of the new investors were from that city. It was doubtful any of them were contemplating a move to Warren and away from their power base. The Warren plant had grown one building at a time as the need for more space became necessary. There was no master plan. A completely new facility would have to be built, and by December 1902 everyone began to realize it was not going to be located in Warren.

Sidney Waldon had been hired as Ward's advertising manager and he took over many of the duties previously handled by George Weiss. He was an extremely competent individual with great imagination. He initiated Packard's first newsletter, *"Strong Talk"* in December containing letters of praise from satisfied customers and followed up with *"Packard Pointers"*, the forerunner of *"The Packard"* magazine. Waldon also encouraged and participated in many publicity events that helped promote the Packard name. He got Joy's attention and became an able assistant to Ward.

Early in December Joy wrote to Ward saying "I am much interested in having your views as to the size and extent of the new factory about which we have talked some,—we are ready to cooperate in [that] manner to the fullest extent. I am strongly in favor of the new plant being built with the knowledge you now have of what such a plant should be. The removal can be accomplished in the [slow] season when the new facility is finished and can be done expediently with a period of shutdown held to a minimum. In order to do this we must act at once preparing plans, specs, and details for new machinery, even though at present some things may not be decided. I urge [your] consideration of these matters because to me they are paramount for the permanent security of our investment and success".

Ward soon asked Henry Joy to send an architect to Warren. The man who arrived in answer to his request was from the office of Albert Kahn. Kahn had remodeled a shop for Henry Boyer, one of the new Packard stockholders and a friend of Henry Joy. It is probable that Joy

The Gene Meador PACKARD agency in San Antonio, Texas. This building was designed by Albert Kahn. Photo taken by Roger T. White in 2000. Main Lincoln Mercury took over this historic structure after the demise of the Packard Motor Car Company, and currently an effort is being made to preserve it for posterity. the carvevd lettering has been highlighted in this photo. The 1936 Packard belongs to Mr. White.

had heard of Kahn's work through him but, however they got together, it is certain that Kahn made a strong impression on Joy. On January 9th, after meeting with him and hearing his ideas, Joy wrote to Ward and announced Kahn had been hired.

Albert Kahn turned out to be the right person for the project at hand. He was an extremely talented and innovative architect and the contract to build the Packard plant, his largest to date, became an important milestone in a brilliant career. This project started his company on the road to international prominence.

Kahn was 33 years old when he was commissioned by Henry Joy to design the Packard plant. Born in a small Westphalian village in Germany, the son of an itinerant Rabbi, Kahn arrived in Detroit with his family in 1884. He attended art classes with Julius Melchors, the city's foremost sculptor. At age twenty-one Kahn won a $1500 traveling scholarship to Europe in a contest sponsored by the *American Architecture Magazine*, and upon his return to Detroit he established his own architectural design office.

The commission to design the new Packard factory from the ground up offered Kahn an opportunity to introduce many innovations in industrial plant design which would become industry guidelines for years to come. He became the architect of choice for Ford, Chrysler and General Motors. It is estimated he designed two billion dollars' worth of factories before his death in 1942—including 150 major plants for General Motors.

In regard to the Packard facility Kahn and Joy were of one mind. Both subscribed to single story facilities with lots of light from above and open floor space for smooth product flow, a concept which unfortunately had to be abandoned in future years due to the lack of space available for expansion. Space, however, was not a problem as the first plans were drawn up since a site had not been determined. Without site restrictions Kahn and Joy had the luxury of designing the ideal factory for the foreseeable future.

Ward was also involved in the planning of the new facility in that he had to decide upon the new machinery requirements and the feasibility of relocating existing equipment. Even before the site was decided upon Joy set a deadline for the move at October 1, 1903. An

Model K with rear entrance — Enhanced photo from 1903 sales catalog.

ambitious schedule to say the least, but one Joy was determined to adhere to.

There was no auto show at the Madison Square Garden in 1902. It had been moved up to the third week in 1903, January 17th to the 24th. Sidney Waldon took over this job which in previous years had been handled by George Weiss. Fred March went with him to help.

The exhibit featured the new Model K, Packard's first four-cylinder car, which Schmidt had been working on since he was first hired the previous April. It attracted great attention but it still had problems. A "new" Model F was also displayed with a longer hood and a few mechanical modifications but little else. The Model G was nowhere to be seen unless one visited the New York showroom on West 59th Street where there were two available for sale. Joy wanted to get rid of these since they were not selling. He even suggested that they might be converted into trucks.

Joy and Ward stopped by the booth at the Garden from time to time as well as the former Adams-McMurtry showroom, which the Packard Motor Car Company had taken over in October 1902.

Joy also wanted Ward to attend a meeting in New York of the Association of Licensed Automobile Manufacturers (the ALAM), a new organization formed to deal with the Electric Vehicle Company, the holder of the Selden Patent. The Association had been formed by the current leaders of the automobile industry, men like Ward Packard, Henry Joy, George Pierce, Elwood Haynes, Edgar Apperson and others in an effort to deal as a body with the royalty claims exercised by Electric Vehicle on behalf of George B. Selden. His patent granted in 1895, covered "gasoline vehicles" in general and was considered invalid by most people because of its ambiguity. Nevertheless, many manufacturers paid the one half of one percent royalty on each unit sold rather than go through the time and expense of legal action. Every Packard automobile carried a Selden Patent plate until 1911 when Henry Ford and some non-ALAM members finally challenged and won a suit against Electric Vehicle Company, invalidating the patent.

Since George Blackmore became the first Packard dealer in September 1900, the number of dealer franchises had been growing at a rate comparable with sales. The Detroit investors were now in complete

Model K—standard model with fixed top and windshield.

control but the city still lacked a Packard agency. Joy and Alger wanted to get Metzger & Company, the agent for Cadillac and Winton among others, to take on Packard. Although Metzger wished to do so, Warren had a backlog in production and they were unable to provide any cars for show. Nevertheless, the situation eased and in April, just before the Detroit Auto Show, Metzger & Company joined the growing list of Packard agencies.

Packard was now represented in some of the most important cities in the nation. After New York (Adams-McMurtry) came Boston (H.B. Shattuck & Son) in April 1901, followed by Buffalo (Ellicott Evans) later that same year. The Pardee Company became the Packard dealer in Chicago in March 1902, their inauguration coinciding with Chicago's first auto show which William Doud attended. Philadelphia (Randolph Winslow) was added to the list in April. During the three years the company had been controlled by the Packard brothers and George Weiss, the founders had built an impressive dealership base representing the company in five major cities. Under Joy and Waldon dealership growth would continue. After Metzger & Company became the Detroit representative in April 1903, the Packard Motor Car Company's strong publicity efforts, under Ward Packard and Sidney Waldon, enticed San Francisco (A.B. Costigan) and Los Angeles (Crippen & Church) to join the growing list of franchisees on the eve of the move to Detroit. Packard dealerships now stretched from coast to coast.

Only the largest Packard agencies have been mentioned here. Several smaller franchises were granted during the same period. C.J. Blousfield of Bay City, Michigan became a dealer in July 1902 and Blackmore was still active in Painesville, Ohio and placing his own ads in *"The Horseless Age"*.

In Warren repercussions were still being felt from the changes mandated on October 13th of the previous year. On January 27, 1903, Hatcher tendered his resignation. Schmidt had taken over many of his duties in April of the previous year and the emphasis in production was changing from single cylinder to four cylinder vehicles. There had been many changes in personnel and undoubtedly he realized there were more to come. Like Weiss he was unhappy and made the decision to move on. His interest in the automobile business stayed with him, however, and after leaving Packard he tried, with a partner named,

Model K chassis.

Francis O. Brew, to manufacture his own automobile in Cleveland. It was called the "Brew-Hatcher", but only a few units were ever produced.

Two days after Hatcher left, on January 29th another special stockholders' meeting was held with the primary purpose of naming a new board of directors as mandated at the previous meeting of October 13th. Only four stockholders were present, William Doud, Ward, and Sidney Waldon from Warren, and Robert Gorton from Detroit, who held proxies for the Detroit investors. As in the meetings of October 13, 1902, everything had been decided upon beforehand. The directors elected, each for a one year term, were the Packard brothers and Waldon from Warren and five investors from Detroit: Joy, Russell Alger, Joseph Boyer, Truman Newberry, and Phillip McMillan.

The Model K, introduced at the Auto Show, received good press. *"The Automobile"* said "its workmanship, design and finish is easily in the front rank of all the American cars shown". They praised the French styling and took note of the price of $7,500, the highest listing of any American car on the market to date.

The Model K wheel base was 91 inches and its four-cylinder engine developed 24 hp. With its sloping Renault-style hood it attracted attention but it had many serious problems which seemed to defy solution. Joy had tried to build interest in multi-cylinder engines well before he gained control of the company but now his pet project seemed to be coming back to haunt him. Joy took his first ride in the experimental model of the K in Warren on February 25th. He was not pleased. Since Ward was not in town at the time Joy wrote him a letter saying "it misses, due to excess of oil in the cylinders, [caused by] the splash feed lubrication. I am and always have been opposed to the splash feed lubrication in the crankcase, although it might be used in Europe. The operation of the `K' machine in Warren was a disgrace to the Packard Company and is better to be scrapped if it cannot be made to run—[splash lubrication] destroys a gasoline engine by getting oil where it is not wanted, on the spark plugs! Do you believe me? I can prove it". In a subsequent letter Joy said he had never seen a Model K run with any satisfaction. These letters undoubtedly upset Ward. He was not used to being treated in this manner and it was in regard to the four-cylinder Model K, a model he never cared for in the first place.

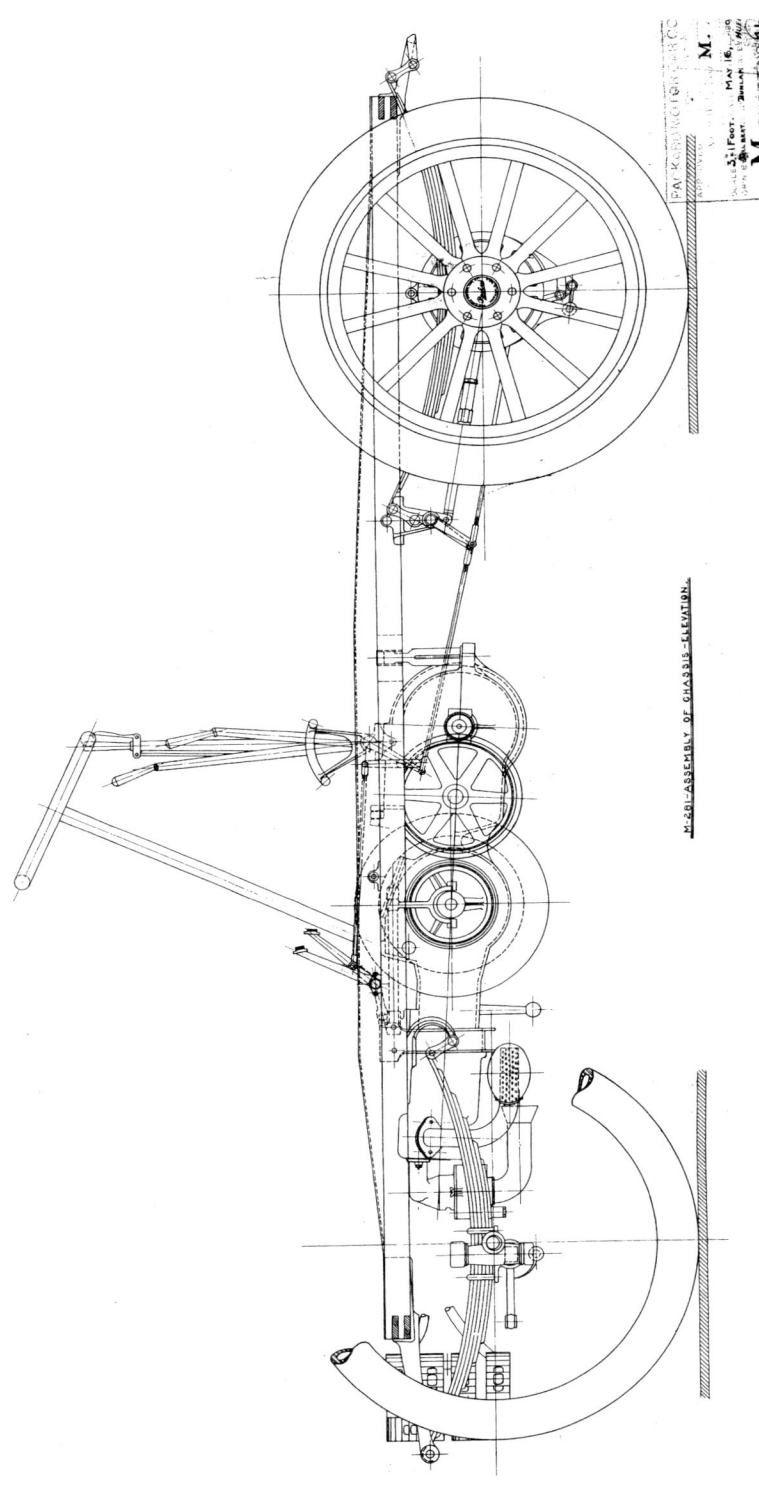

Model M—left side view—copy from original print. Prototype was built, but it never went into production.

Chapter 6 - the Move to Detroit

He wrote back to Joy claiming the `K' was not a splash feed, but Joy contradicted him again and was at least partially right. The `K' did have a dash mounted oiler which had to be refilled periodically since there was no oil pump. After the oiler had released its contents into the crankcase the splash action was the only lubrication the engine received unless the oiler was refilled manually.

The problems with the `K' were to continue well into the summer, which must have overwhelmed Schmidt. Some relief came when C.J. Moore of Westfield, Massachusetts was hired as factory manager on March 8th. He, like Schmidt, was a man of real ability who would prove to be instrumental in solving some of the problems of the `K' and other new models in the works while still maintaining production of the ever popular `F', the only financially profitable product they had.

At the beginning of 1903 the most popular automobiles were still the single cylinder machines. The `F' proved that and on the streets of Detroit Joy could see lots of the little single cylinder curved dash Oldsmobiles. These simple vehicles made a big hit with the people who were not able to spend $7,500 or even $2,500, the price of an `F', to get rid of their horse.

On February 5th at the first board meeting held in Detroit the Model M had been approved to compete with the curved dash Oldsmobiles. Although it was an idea that Ward may have liked, it seems to have originated with Joy. Whether the idea was good or not is a question that can't be answered. The 'M', a 14 hp one-cylinder engine, cooled by water, passing through the cylinder casting, which eliminated the need for the copper jacket used on the Model F, a change which was probably made as a cost-saving feature.

Regardless of Joy's letters, original engine drawings exist showing that the `M' finally emerged as a two-cylinder machine, with horizontal "siamesed" cylinders (the `G' had opposed cylinders) and it had a light carriage. The design of the engine block required complicated internal coring because of the elimination of the copper water jacket. This in turn complicated the casting process and increased costs. The engine configuration in the chassis was very similar to the Model F design. In all probability the two-cylinder paired engine contributed to the failure of the project because of excessive vibration —- they didn't know how to effectively counterbalance an engine of this type in 1903.

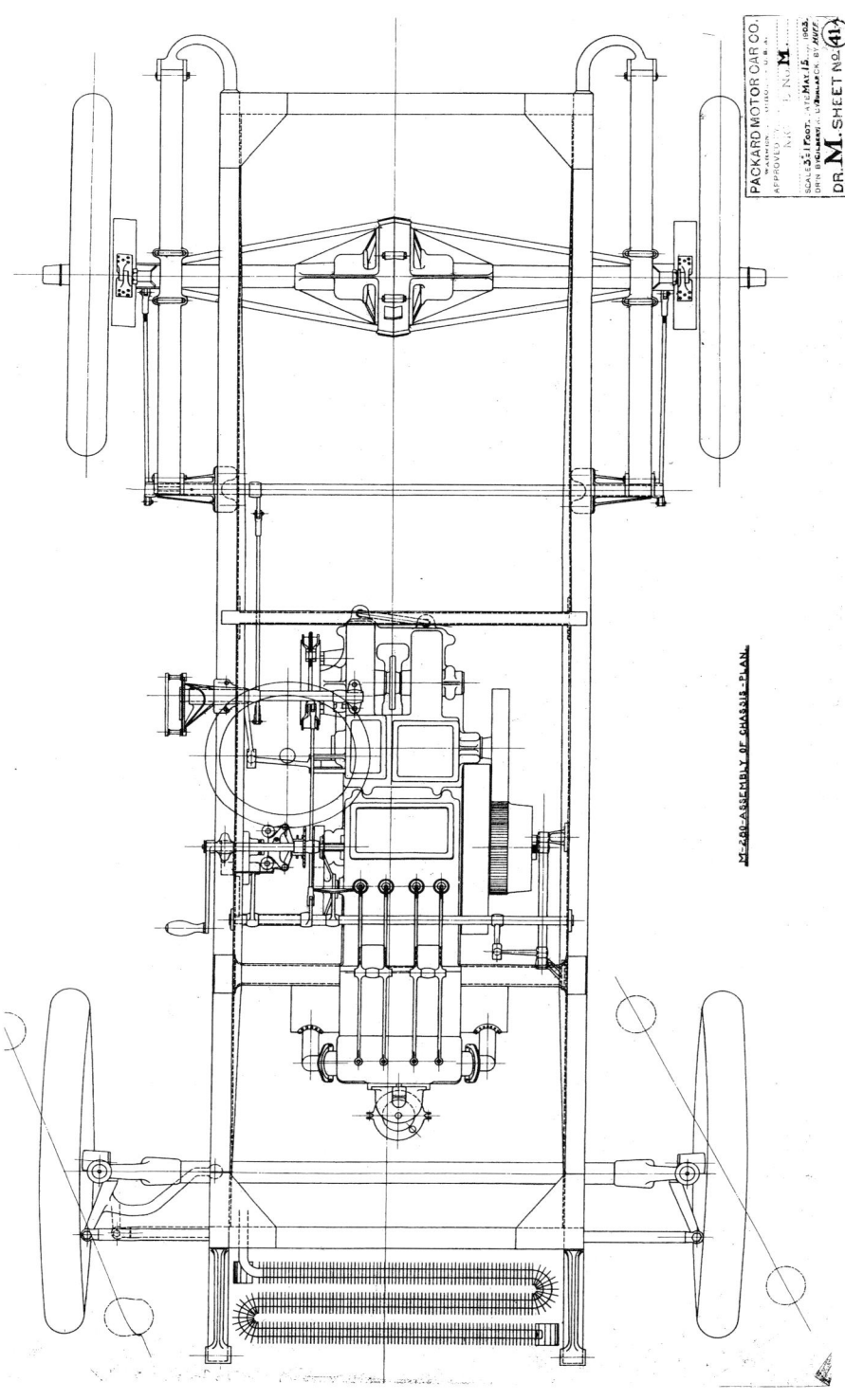

Model M—copy of original print. Top view showing the two-cylinder, siamesed horizontal engine.

Chapter 6 - the Move to Detroit

On March 10th Joy asked Ward to make some sketches for `M' bodies. He wrote "No possible effort [should] be spared to make this machine pleasing to the eye and easy to manipulate and in fact [it should be] a jewel which at a glance a person will say 'there is the most attractive thing I have ever seen'. You can do this if you will – such is my firm faith in you". After Joy's harsh letters to Ward a little over a week before in which he criticized the troublesome Model K, he seemed to be trying to make amends.

Later in March, seemingly still enthusiastic about the 'M' Joy wrote, "I feel our next vehicle must be a two-seated type runabout. If we can [produce] such a machine, and get it right, use a single cylinder like the Olds, it would be an excellent car. Sell it for $900 to $1000 suitable for physicians or businessmen's use. I feel we can make a machine far better than any on the market today".

On April 9th Joy wrote that he was anxious to go to Warren and see the `M' as soon as it was completed. But throughout April the factory had problems finding a foundry capable of making the more complicated water-cooled cylinder castings. This delayed work on the project. Finally Joy wrote to Moore, the new plant manager, and asked him to talk to Schmidt about changing the design to use a copper jacket like the `F'. In the meantime Joy arranged to have castings made in Detroit.

The delays, however, were having an effect on Joy's attitude toward the project. He wrote on May 7th that it was okay to make up a few more machines but noted that Newberry and Alger thought the `M' should not be offered for sale at all during the current year.

It was May 21st before Ward reported the `M' was "out and running". By June 9th, however, only one `M' had been tested and James Ward noted "it was not very promising". He sent a report to Joy who replied that "the difficulties enumerated in the `M' machine lead to the conclusion that the proper machine is the four-cylinder vertical, where there is a proper place for everything and everything can be in its place". The `M' was now a thing of the past.

Plans for the new plant had been completed by May 19th when the board of directors approved the purchase of 66.4 acres of undeveloped land Joy had selected outside of the Detroit city limits. On that date when

Model K with side entrance to back seats, sold to William Rockefeller.

Chapter 6 - the Move to Detroit

the board approved the payment of $19,434 for the acreage it also authorized the purchase of a strip of land to be used to connect the factory to the Michigan Central Railway. The size of the site was considerably larger than was needed to accommodate the factory envisioned in Albert Kahn's design, which left room for future growth.

With expenses relating to the new factory rising and only the Model F sales as income Joy decided that it would be necessary to borrow money to build the new facility rather than delay the move to Detroit which was still planned for October. On June 16th the board approved Kahn's final plans and specifications as well as the contracts to build the plant in accordance with Joy's proposals for financing. The firm of Teakle and Golden of Detroit was selected to build the plant at a cost not to exceed $117,309, plus $5000 for washroom fittings. They guaranteed to complete the facility, four times the size of the Warren plant, within four months. The October deadline for moving was still in sight.

Meanwhile in Warren the infamous `K' was still proving to be a headache for all concerned. Schmidt was dedicating most of his time to the `K' project. Joy was under the impression that the problems would eventually be solved and felt the need to continue its promotion. Sooner or later they would have to be sold to recoup their investment. In April he had asked to have K No. 1 sent to Detroit for publicity purposes. He also ordered another `K' for delivery by June 1st which he planned to take along when he went on vacation in July at the family summer home at Watch Hill, Rhode Island.

W.S. Ions drove K No.1 to Detroit. He had problems but he got there. Joy tinkered with the car himself and still was dissatisfied. Tom Fetch was sent to Detroit and seemed to have a little better luck. The `K' ran better for a few days and then dropped its drive shaft. Schmidt had an explanation which Joy did not accept. He wrote back to Ward, "The shaft is insufficiently keyed for a transmission of so much power. I would hope you would remedy the problem before you sell one of these cars. It must be on the others already out". Ward's nerves were now on edge. Warren had delivered several `K's—defects and all.

Truman Newberry had taken delivery of another Model K and driven it east to Watch Hill. Joy wrote Ward with the familiar news, "The drive shaft dropped out—twice".

Although no original production K's exist, this notorious vehicle is still of interest to collectors. Mr. Willis Boyd of Escondido, CA, built this meticulously accurate replica from original blueprints. Only the engine has been slightly modified to make the car more roadworthy.

Chapter 6 - the Move to Detroit

Newberry also wrote to Ward concerning the incident. It is not known exactly what was said in the letter or how it was phrased, but for Ward it was the last straw. On July 18, 1903, James Ward Packard wrote in his diary: "Letter from Newberry today caused me to decide to withdraw from the Packard Motor Car Company".

James Ward, of course, had been unhappy for some time. Even though he was "President" he had not exercised any executive authority since the October 13th board meeting. Joy had been issuing the orders since that date and sometimes in a not too diplomatic way. Joy was not an easy man to get along with. In fact, Ward had already read a statement of resignation, as president, to the board on June 16th, one month earlier when he realized he had almost no control over the work being done in Warren.

It wasn't long before Henry Joy learned of Ward's decision. To Truman Newberry he wrote: "I hardly know how to express my feeling in regard to your action in writing such a letter as you did to the Packard Motor Car Company at Warren—It seems to me that you have taken the function of the board into your [own] hands by having written such a letter—insulting Mr. Packard and throwing aside all due regard to whether or not your associates might wish to drive Mr. Packard out of the company, which is the effect your letter had".

Russell Alger was sent to Warren to try to sooth Ward's feelings and change his mind. Ward told Alger, "I will continue for the present". That didn't satisfy Joy, so he wrote Ward a personal letter: "I can only state to you that I have never been so shocked and so severely chagrined that any of my associates should write such a letter as this to you with utter disregard for decency, not only with reference to you but to [plant superintendent] Moore, and your company. I can not find words to express to you how deeply I feel about the matter and your efforts for the company against your will. I have the greatest respect for you...."

What was meant by "efforts for the company against your will"? Did this allude to the resistance on the part of Ward towards the four-cylinder cars—the move to Detroit—or just a general dissatisfaction with the policies forced upon him in Warren? The answers to these questions will never be known. There was only one thing for sure—James Ward Packard was not a happy man in his present position.

Two views of the updated 1903 Model F. Note the more attractive radiator and the gas, oil, and water caps integrated into the hood. This seemingly convenient freature was later discontinued because road vibration caused them to leak and come apart.

Chapter 6 - the Move to Detroit

Even with the new 32,000 square foot building, which went into service in January 1903, the Warren work load was overwhelming. Six different models were in the process of being designed, built or tested during the first nine months of 1903. They were the F, G, K, M and L. Unfortunately, the `F' was the only one paying its way. Model Fs were produced throughout 1902 and most of 1903. 'F' production ended when the Warren plant closed in October 1903. They were classified by their model years. All `F's were of the same basic design although there were slight differences between the 1902 and the 1903 models. According to the Packard Historical "Hand Book", Number 3, issued May, 1911, Model F production was 100 units in 1902 and 144 units in 1903 - a total production of 244 Model Fs.

By July the 'G' and 'M had been discontinued and the `K's being produced were not fulfilling their promise. The Model L, the second four-cylinder Packard and the first one to be built in Detroit was still in the design stages.

In addition to the manufacturing operations in Warren, Waldon and Ward were continually involved with the advertising and promotion of the company.

When Dr. Horatio Nelson Jackson from Burlington, Vermont, along with his mechanic Sewall K. Crocker, drove from San Francisco to New York in a used two-cylinder Winton, Ward and Waldon decided it was time for them to get into the act. It would be good publicity for Packard to do so.

Jackson had made the sixty three day trip on a bet and threw a rod in the process. Some people said that the Winton was helped over some of the more difficult stretches of the trip by railroad, but this was denied. Winton offered a $10,000 reward for anyone who could prove this and Dr. Jackson added another $15,000. The reward was never claimed.

Even before the Winton trip Joy had written to Waldon about the need for advertising that would keep the Packard name "on top" and mentioned that he talked with Alger "relative to the cross country trip Waldon and Mr. Packard have had in mind for so long".

Flat tires plagued Fetch and Krarup during their transcontinental trip, but they made it in 61 days, three days less than Jackson's time in his Winton.

The Sunday after chucrch crowd, admiring Old Pacific at Manatou Springs, Colorado.

Chapter 6 - the Move to Detroit

With everyone's blessing a Model F was taken from stock and with a few modifications, including extra fuel tanks and a lower first gear, was prepared for shipment to San Francisco. Tom Fetch was selected to drive the car along with a guide to lead the way across the wilderness. At the last minute the guide failed to show up and Marius C. Krarup, the editor of *"The Automobile"*, who was on hand to cover the start from San Francisco, stepped up to take his place. He proved to be an asset as a publicist even though he was a failure as a guide. They took over 750 photographs during the trip and received great press coverage from coast to coast.

They started on June 20, 1903, at 5:00 p.m. from the Cliff House, in view of the Pacific Ocean, with great fanfare. The first leg of their journey followed the Union Pacific railroad and as they headed up over the Sierra Nevada range they decided to name their Packard "Old Pacific".* The name stuck and their trip became a major publicity triumph for the Packard Motor Car Company. They were well received by curious crowds all along the route and their progress was followed closely by the newspapers nationwide. Although the projected distance to New York was only 3,000 miles they had driven 5,600 miles before they reached their destination, having made several side trips and getting lost from time to time! On August 21st, after 61 days on the road, they received a tumultuous welcome upon their arrival in New York. "Old Pacific", their single cylinder Model F, had completed the epic journey without any serious mechanical problems. Ward and Sidney Waldon were elated, Tom Fetch and Marius Krarup were just tired.

As "Old Pacific" was making headlines the Model K and its related problems were still uppermost in the minds of Ward and Waldon. In spite of the failures related to the `K' it had some redeeming features and of course it had to be marketed. The company was betting its future on the four cylinder vehicles. There was no turning back.

From the very beginning the 25 hp `K' showed that it had a capability for more speed than any of the previous models. Early in the year the board had authorized the construction of a `K' as a racing car and it became Schmidt's favorite project. It had a slightly larger bore than the stock model, two forward speeds, no reverse gear and an

* "Old Pacific" is currently on display at the Henry Ford Museum in Dearborn, Michigan.

The Gray Wolf—designed in Warren by Charles Schmidt, seen here in the driver's seat.

Chapter 6 - the Move to Detroit

aluminum body. All these modifications were made to reduce the weight and improve the weight-to-horsepower ratio. The K Special weighed only 1310 lbs. in relation to the stock Model K, which tipped the scales at 2200 lbs. It was called the K Special and Ward worked closely with Schmidt in preparing for its debut. Ward invited Henry Joy to see the car on July 30th when it had its first trial run. On August 8th it was taken to the Warren fairground for another run and Ward clocked the mile at 1:26.

When the time came to introduce the K Special to the public an exhibition run was scheduled for August 28th at the Trumbull County Fair Grounds, near Warren. As an added attraction Tom Fetch was there with "Old Pacific", having just returned from his transcontinental trip the previous week. Schmidt completed ten laps around the half-mile track and his best time for a one mile stretch was 1:16 minutes – an excellent showing the `K' and the Company could be proud of. The *Cleveland Plain Dealer* had a reporter present who referred to the K Special as the "Gray Wolf" and the name stuck.

The "Gray Wolf" had an illustrious career over the next two years with Schmidt as its principal driver. It was pitted against the best cars and drivers of the day; Barney Oldfield in the Winton Bullet #2 and Tom Cooper in Ford's 999. Harry Cunningham took Schmidt's place at times and the Gray Wolf maintained its place among the star contenders. It won races and broke records at speeds over 70 mph but it was a time when automobile development was moving forward at a phenomenal pace and no car or driver held the top position very long. Nevertheless, the Gray Wolf earned its place in history and helped keep the Packard name fixed in the eyes of the public well beyond 1903.

After Ward let it be known on July 18th that he intended to "withdraw from the Packard Motor Car Company", there was a concerted effort on the part of Newberry and Alger to get Joy to officially take over the management of the company. Nevertheless, he left for Watch Hill without resolving the situation which contributed to the confusion in Warren. Joy's secretary wrote him saying that even Ward and Waldon wanted him to take over the reigns. It was clear that Ward was fed up with the existing management ambiguity, and even though he had told Alger he would "stay for now," he didn't say in what capacity. It was obvious to all Joy had unofficially taken over the management of the company months before —now it was time to make it official.

The Model L designed in Warren—and the first model produced in Detroit.

Chapter 6 - the Move to Detroit

On September 8, 1903, new officers were elected, with Russell Alger being name vice president and Phillip H. McMillan becoming the secretary-treasurer. James Ward was again named president. It seems Joy and the board of directors had concluded that Ward Packard should retain the presidency of the Packard Motor Car Company, even though the position by this time had become in all respects an "honorary" one. It was a title which would be continually conferred upon him through 1909. The big news, however, was recorded in Ward's diary on September 11, 1903, when he stated Joy had arrived in Warren to "take full charge of the PMCC".

"Old Pacific" and the "Gray Wolf" certainly provided the highlights in an otherwise dismal year for the factory in Warren. The problems with the Model K and its failure as a saleable product were a source of frustration and discouragement for all concerned. Even though the unreliable four had been his idea, Joy finally concluded, "The K machine ——- is simply a disgrace to the company".

On the bright side the problems encountered with the `K' were ultimately addressed in the Model L, Packard's first successful four cylinder car. The design of the `L' model had been authorized by the board at the February 5th meeting along with the ill-fated, two-cylinder `M'. Charles Schmidt was in charge of the design of both models and when the board decided to discontinue work on the `M' in favor of the `L', on June 11th, he was able to concentrate his efforts on two similar designs, one of which was already in limited production and exhibited obvious defects. The flaws in the `K' were corrected in the `L', the first model to be produced in Detroit and an automobile that proved to be a credit to the company.

In spite of valiant efforts to save the `K' it continued to be a source of embarrassment. Sidney Waldon reported in 1911 that the company had imported the best foreign engineering talent it could find and gave that talent a free rein, with the result that the company had to buy back and scrap every one of the twenty-five Model Ks sold. Packard had many automotive industry firsts to be proud of, but without a doubt having the first "recall" was not one of them.

The Model K debacle was a hard lesson for the company. To make sure it was never repeated The Packard Experimental Department was formed immediately after the move to Detroit. This effort was led by

Packard Motor Car Company

MAIN OFFICE & WORKS,
WARREN, OHIO.

WARREN, OHIO. Oct. 3, 1903.

Mr. George Weiss,
   75 Ingleside Ave.,
      Cleveland, Ohio.

> AFTER OCTOBER 10
> Address All Communications
> PACKARD MOTER CAR COMPANY,
> Detroit, Mich.

Dear Sir:---

    We wish to call your attention to the notice of change of address which we are placing on this letter. We will be located at our new factory at Detroit, Michigan, the latter part of the next week. We trust that you will bear this in mind and any communications which you may send us, please address to that city, on and about Oct. 10.

    The amount of work involved in moving our entire plant and offices to our new factory is enormous. Should any correspondence not receive as prompt attention as usual for a few days, we trust that you will appreciate the conditions.

                     Very respectfully,
                     PACKARD MOTOR CAR COMPANY
                               W. R. D.

WRD-B

Change of address letter received by George Weiss. It was written on light blue letterhead stationery on October third and updated with a white sticker opposite the recipient's name at the last minute.

Chapter 6 - the Move to Detroit

Russell Huff who had joined the company in 1900. He had become assistant engineer under Schmidt and rose to chief engineer in January 1905 when Schmidt left Packard to join the Peerless Motor Car Company in Cleveland.

Joy was in Warren on September 11th planning the closure of the facility. On September 14th the *"Warren Chronicle"* reported, "this morning [the company] began tearing out machines for shipment to Detroit". The company had approximately 300 employees at that time and although a few quit many decided to make the move with the company.

In Detroit the rush was on to receive the influx from Warren on October 15th. C.J. Moore, as plant manager, was trying to get everything ready for a smooth transition. But as of September 30th things were still in a state of flux. No steam would be available for three weeks, sprinkler and heating systems were inoperable and mud hampered movement throughout the plant site and adjoining roads. Nevertheless, Joy was determined to keep to his schedule.

All office equipment, records and furniture were to be shipped as of October 10th and W.D. Densmore, of Warren, was told several days before to prepare a small sticker, with a forwarding address, to be placed on all outgoing correspondence. It read:

AFTER OCTOBER 10
Address All Communications
PACKARD MOTER CAR COMPANY
Detroit, Mich.

(Mr. Densmore obviously had a problem with his spelling!)

The *"Warren Chronicle"* confirmed the shipment of the office furniture and the departure of many Packard employees for Detroit on Saturday, October 10th, thus ending the Warren era of the Packard automobile.

On Thursday, October 8th James Ward Packard was in Detroit attending the last board meeting prior to the start of operations in the new plant. Early the following morning he received word that his mother, who was seemingly healthy, had died suddenly during the night. Ward

The new Packard Motor Car Co. plant, Detroit, Michigan, October 1903.

Chapter 6 - the Move to Detroit

left for Warren immediately. The family gathered for the funeral on Sunday morning. It had been a difficult weekend for the Packard family and the city of Warren. Ward and W.D. had lost their mother and the Packard plant was gone.

Although Ward Packard visited the factory in Detroit occasionally after the move was completed, he never again was active in the administration of the company. The title of "president", which he held until 1909, was strictly honorary.

The move to Detroit was indeed a difficult time for all concerned but, after a short period of consolidation and the introduction of the very successful Model L, the company was once again at the forefront of the luxury automobile market. Within two years the Packard Motor Car Company was making a profit and there would be no more financial worries for the next twenty-five years.

Although he could be criticized for his management style, Henry Joy was a resolute leader with a clear sense of direction. He built a strong management team that maintained the standard of quality set by the founders.

As in many emerging companies, the men with the original ideas passed from the scene and others with both money and vision took over and transformed a small company into a large prominent corporation. Henry Joy did well for Packard. It is doubtful the company could have retained its position in the industry without his personal and financial influence.

James Ward Packard with wife Elizabeth Gillmer Packard in their 1904 Model L during their honeymoon trip to Lake Chautagua, New York in September 1904.
Photo taken at Panama Rocks near the lake.

Epilogue (Part I)

James Ward Packard
(1863-1928)

The decisions that culminated in the removal of the Packard Motor Car Company from Warren, Ohio, to Detroit, Michigan, in 1903, had a career-altering effect on James Ward Packard, the guiding genius who had developed the Packard automobile. Nominally still the company president, Packard was removed from the general management of the operation when Henry B. Joy became the new general manager in Detroit. It was no doubt a depressing time of introspection for a person who possessed such creative talents and interests.

James Ward Packard continued as vice president and general manager of the New York & Ohio Company with its incandescent lamp production and as president of the Packard Electric Company where his research and development skills led the company into the production of automotive harnesses. In 1906, James Ward Packard withdrew as the Packard Electric general manager, turning this position over to a fellow Lehigh University alumnus, Newton A. Wolcott of Farmington in Trumbull County.

In the summer of 1904, James Ward Packard informed his brother that he planned to marry. William Doud obtained the marriage license for his brother, listing him as "retired" (at age 40). The bride was Elizabeth A. Gillmer, daughter of Trumbull County Common Pleas Judge Thomas I. Gillmer. She was a Vassar graduate, had taught school briefly, and did volunteer work at the Warren Library. The couple shared a common interest in the intellectual pursuits and treasures the library could provide. It helped that her father was also head of the library association. The wedding took place at the Gillmer home on High Street on August 31, 1904. Following the ceremony, the newlyweds left for a honeymoon in Lakewood, New York, in the groom's Packard.

By 1906, the *Warren City Directory* listed James Ward Packard with Lakewood, New York, as a primary residence with Mr. and Mrs. Packard identifying the Packard Block on Courthouse Square as their Warren home. In 1902 James Ward Packard had built Warren's first modern apartment building on Park Avenue. "The Packard" as it was called, was designed by John Eisenmann of Cleveland, architect of the Cleveland Arcade building and creator of Ohio's State Flag. Several members of the Packard family had apartments there.

In 1908 Packard purchased the Abell homestead, that had been built in 1837 on Park Avenue (known as Liberty Street in its early days). The interior was remodeled to reflect the Packards' interests. This historic dwelling survives as the Buckeye Club for Warren, Ohio, professional people.

In 1909 James Ward Packard had relinquished his completely "honorary title" as president of the Packard Motor Car Company. In 1911, while still serving as president of the Packard Electric Company, he built a new summer residence in Lakewood on the site of the Packard family's original summer home. The old frame dwellings were moved to new locations nearby where they have recently been restored.

1915 also saw the gift of land and construction funds for the Lakewood, New York Village Hall. Another gift was a Model T Ford fire truck. This restored fire engine is the prized possession of the current Lakewood Fire Department.

Boating on Lake Chautauqua, collecting clocks and watches, and collecting various types of firearms were James Ward Packard's primary hobby interests. He maintained a keen interest in all things mechanical. In 1922, James Ward Packard commissioned the Patek, Philippe & Company of Geneva, Switzerland, to make an amazing astronomical watch with a celestial chart, showing over 500 stars in six different sizes according to magnitude and calculated for the latitude of Warren, Ohio, (42 degrees 20 minutes). This masterpiece took five years to complete and cost 12,815 Swiss francs. Packard was the leading American collector of Patek, Philippe watches. In 1994, the watch company repurchased the Packard timepiece for a record $1.3 million. This famed watch is on display at the Patek, Philippe Museum in Geneva, Switzerland.

A new winter home in the new Oak Knoll subdivision on Warren's east side was completed in 1924. In Lakewood, charitable giving continued during 1925, including chimes and a church bell for the Methodist Church there and a $150,000 donation toward a new wing for the Jamestown, New York, hospital.

Epilogue (Part I) — James Ward Packard (1863-1928)

In January 1926, James Ward Packard entered George Crile's Cleveland Clinic where surgery was performed on the 26th. Initial newspaper reports of his recovery were optimistic but James Ward Packard remained in Cleveland for further treatment. The cancer had spread to other parts of his body. Packard made a philanthropic gift of $200,000 to the Cleveland Clinic for medical research. This gift included 5,000 shares of Packard Motor Car Company stock valued at $30 a share. Others would benefit from his generous donation.

As part of a 1926 Warren Elks Club project, James Ward Packard purchased the Pine Street location which would become the first permanent home of the Salvation Army in Warren. Also in 1926, he donated $55,000 for the enlargement of the Warren Public Library. New equipment and furnishings were included. The Packard gift doubled Andrew Carnegie's 1904 donation to construct the original library. The James Ward Packard Reading Room now houses the Trumbull County Law Library collection of about 32,000 hardbound books. The building was restored in 1996.

A carillon and stained glass window, in honor of his mother, was a gift to Christ Episcopal Church of Warren. The capstone of his philanthropy during his lifetime was a $1,000,000 gift for an engineering building at his alma mater, Lehigh University, in Bethlehem, PA. The first Packard automobile was presented to the university for permanent display by the Packard Motor Car Company after James Ward Packard's death.

James Ward Packard died on March 20, 1928, at the Cleveland Clinic. His death was front page news in Warren and Detroit. *The Warren Tribune Chronicle* eulogized Packard as "a man loved and respected by all who had the privilege of knowing him. Mr. Packard's whole life was an asset to the world and very especially to his home community".

In death, various trusts and endowments were established in his will for the benefit of the Warren Episcopal Church, the Warren Library Association, Warren City Hospital, Lehigh University, and the Seamen's Church Institute of New York City. James Ward Packard's personal libraries were given to the Warren Public Library.

Mrs. Packard continued to live in Lakewood where she served on the board of education, the Jamestown hospital board, and various community organizations. Elizabeth Gillmer Packard died on January 19, 1960 at age 88. She is buried in Warren's Oakwood Cemetery beside her husband.

In his 1925-1926 diaries, James Ward Packard identifies the various Packard automobiles which were housed in his Park Avenue carriage house and his Oak Knoll garage: a Model 226 two passenger Coupe, a Model 326 Coupe, a Model 333 Sedan, a Model 236 Roadster, and a Model 243 Club Sedan. The diary entry on the last named vehicle reads as follows: "Took delivery of a 243 Club Sedan W4573, W.B. 143, cyl. 3 3/8 x 5, H.P. 36.4 displacement 357.65 Motor # 217199A Vehicle # 217199". James Ward Packard's genius for detail had never waned.

Epilogue (Part II)
William Doud Packard
(1861-1923)

1903. It was the year of "Old Pacific" and the Gray Wolf" for the Packard Motor Car Company. The corporate changes had been duly noted in William Doud Packard's diary (along with the notation that founding partner George Lewis Weiss had resigned from the board of directors and as company vice president on November 15, 1902.

On May 12, 1903, the inevitable announcement was contained in the diary entry: "James Ward Packard back from Detroit – decision to build the Motor Car Company in Detroit". In the months that followed, the business of the New York & Ohio Company and the Packard Electric Company continued as usual. On a family note, Mary Elizabeth Doud Packard, mother of the Packard brothers, died on October 9, 1903, after becoming ill at a church function in Warren. She was buried in Lordstown at the Paltzgroff Cemetery next to her mother Anna Paltzgroff Doud Foulk.

William Doud Packard married on June 11, 1891, at Middleton, Connecticut. He wedded Annie Hadley Storer in an elaborate church ceremony at the Church of the Holy Trinity. The wedding party included his sister Alaska Packard and her future husband E.B. McCrum, Jr.

After only four years of marriage Annie Storer Packard died on June 28, 1895, in Warren, Ohio, from complications associated with appendicitis. She was 28 years old. William and Annie had a son, Warren Packard II, who was born on October 5, 1892. He died in an air crash of his Moth seaplane on August 26, 1929, at Grosse Point, Michigan. Warren had served in the Naval Air Corps during World War I.

William Doud Packard remarried on September 27, 1906. He married Kathryn Bruder of Niles and Warren in a quiet ceremony at the Packard family summer residence in Lakewood, New York. They resided at "Rivers Court", the new home he had built on Mahoning Avenue in Warren.

1904 brought the affiliation of the New York and Ohio Company lamp business with the National Electric Lamp Association (NELA) – that became General Electric in later years. William Doud Packard continued as secretary-treasurer of the Ohio Lamp Works (formerly the New York & Ohio Co.) and served as president of the company in 1911 – the year that the city of Warren installed the first incandescent street lights in the nation. He was also a member of the board of directors of the Western Reserve National Bank in Warren.

In 1911, William Doud Packard added "philanthropist" to his role as an industrialist and community leader in his hometown of Warren, Ohio. When a state selection committee chose a Kent, Ohio, site for a state normal school (later Kent State University) over the Kinsman farm site in Warren, Packard purchased the Mahoning Avenue location and donated the property to the city for a public park. Packard Park was officially dedicated on Monday, July 5, 1915. Among its many features was the Japanese Tea Garden – the first such landscape design in the United States east of San Francisco. Over the remaining years of his life, William Doud Packard took a personal interest in the further development of the park. He added a closed shelter house and an amphitheater that was a perfect setting for outdoor summer concerts. Packard's favorite local band, the Black Hussars directed by B.D. Gilliland, gave the first park concert in 1912. Gilliland was well known locally as a trumpeter with the famed Sousa Band.

In 1914, William Doud Packard built a country estate at a cost of $175,000 on the northern edge of the Chautauqua Institute grounds on Lake Chautauqua in New York. In 1919, he also built "Packard Place", a similar brick home for his winter residence in Warren, at a cost of $75,000.

In 1916, the Packard Electric Company was reorganized under the leadership of Newton A. Wolcott who had acquired the Packard interests in the enterprise. Wolcott, a Lehigh University graduate, had joined the company in 1903 and served as general manager since 1906. His new responsibilities included serving as president and treasurer as well as general manager. At the time of Wolcott's death in 1933, the company had become a division of General Motors (now Delphi Packard Electric).

In spite of paralysis and the increasing loss of his eyesight during his last years, William Doud Packard maintained a vital interest in the civic affairs of his community. In his Last Will and Testament, Packard established the Packard Trust to construct a music hall and fund

Epilogue (Part II) — William Doud Packard (1861-1923)

a permanent band organization to provide free public concerts in Warren. He died on November 11, 1923, and is buried on the family lot of Warren's Oakwood Cemetery along with other family members. His wife, Kathryn B. Packard, died on February 10, 1940. Following wartime delays, the W.D. Packard Music Hall was finally built in Packard Park. The first concert by the W.D. Packard Concert Band was performed on October 15, 1955. The fiftieth anniversary concert was celebrated on October 15, 2005.

The William Doud Packard estate included 2,250 shares of preferred stock and 48,000 shares of common stock in the Packard Motor Car Company. Among his other stock holdings were 204 shares of General Electric stock, 150 shares of Pullman Company stock, 260 shares in the Western Reserve National Bank of Warren. At his death, Packard owned a 1918 Packard automobile, Brougham type, Motor # 148616, valued at $500.

The historic legacy and contributions of the Packard family continue to play an important role in the heritage of their hometown of Warren, Ohio.

Epilogue (Part III)
George Lewis Weiss
(1862-1945)

After he resigned his position as vice president and director of the Packard Motor Car Company, Weiss remained active in automotive affairs. He was a member of the Vanderbilt Cup Commission in 1904 and 1905 and he was involved with auto racing at Daytona Beach from its inception.

In 1905 George L. Weiss moved from 75 Ingleside Dr. to a much larger home at 2460 Edgehill Rd., Euclid Heights, Ohio. There he had a garage and shop capable of housing several cars. On March 30th of that year he traded his Packard Motor Car Co. stock for 12 Model Ls which he sold from his Cleveland home.

In succeeding years, as the shares of the company soared in value, he must have suffered from great mental anguish due to this unfortunate decision. He certainly missed the financial windfall of Packard's golden years.

Nevertheless, he moved on to other endeavors that were financially rewarding. In 1907 he became manager and vice president of the American Railroad Signal Co. which later became part of the Westinghouse Corp. His next position was that of a director and manager of the Butler Drawbar and Attachment Co. The company, at that time, held the patent to the railroad car couplings that are still used today. These novel devices are used to connect the rolling stock on trains in all of North America and most of the Western Hemisphere. When the company patents expired after World War I the company sold its remaining product lines and went out of business. Weiss retired comfortably in 1919 at the age of 59 years.

After his retirement, the Weiss family began spending the winter months in Pasadena, California. George Weiss became enamored with Southern California. He persuaded his mother and her sister to move to Long Beach, California in 1920. By 1924 Weiss, his wife, along with their son's family had joined in the move west. Shortly after the move to California, his son, Harold, went to work for Walter McCarty in his speculative real estate venture which became Beverly Hills. George Weiss invested in the McCarty partnership. After a couple of years in Long Beach both families built homes in Beverly Hills and relocated.

George Weiss lived in Beverly Hills the rest of his life, but he and his wife kept their ties with Cleveland and made frequent summer trips east by train. Their grandson, Roger, who wrote the Foreword for this book, used to join them on these annual pilgrimages.

George Lewis Weiss died September 27, 1945, at the age of 83. He is buried at Lakeview Cemetery, Cleveland, Ohio.p

Appendix A

New York Packard Agent Addresses
Taken from Magazine Ads
Feb 6, 1901 to June 13, 1903

Date	Recorded New York Address
Feb. 6, 1901	Eastern Sales Office, George B. Adams, Mgr
April 3, 1901	114 5th Avenue, NY
July, 1901	Eastern Dept. The Adams-McMurtry Co.
November, 1901	114 5th Avenue, NY
Nov. 13, 1901	Eastern Sales Dept. Adams-McMurtry Co. 114 5th Avenue & 7 East 28th St., NY
Dec. 4, 1901	Eastern Dept., Adams-McMurtry Co. 114 5th Avenue, NY
Dec. 11, 1901	Adams-McMurtry Co. moved to a new facility
Dec. 18, 1901	Eastern Dept., Adams-McMurtry Co. 317-319 West 59th St. NY
Jan. 23, 1902	Eastern Dept., Adams-McMurtry Co. 317 West 59th St., NY
Aug. 18, 1902	Adams-McMurtry Co. sold to the Packard Motor Car Co.
December 1902	Eastern Dept., George B. Adams, Mgr. 317 W. 59th St. NY
January 1903	Eastern Dept
June 13, 1903	317 W. 59th St., NY

From this time forward ads read: "Write for name of nearest agent".

Appendix B

PRODUCTION OF MODELS A and B in WARREN

Packard & Weiss Partnership

The First Packard		Nov. 6, 1899
A 21	W.D. Packard	April (?) 1900
A 22	G.L. Weiss	April 20, 1900
A 23	George Kirkham	May 2, 1900
A 24	Charles G. Harris	May 7, 1900
A 25	Fred W. Harris	May 17, 1900
B 26	August Veghte	June 20, 1900
B 27	John F. McNutt	June 21, 1900
B 28	A.F. Harris	July 11, 1900
B 29	? J.W. Packard	Aug. 20, 1900
B 30	George Blackmore	Aug. ? 1900

Ohio Automobile Co. formed — September 10, 1900

B 31	? Dr. S.P. Ecki	Sept. - 3rd week
B 32		
B 33		
B 34		
B 35		
B 36		
B 37		
B 38		
B 38		
B 39	National Auto Museum, Reno, Nevada	
B 40		
B 41		
B 42		
B 43		
B 44		
B 45		
B 46		
B 47		
B 48		
B 49		
B 50		
B 51		
B 52		
B 53		
B 54	The last Model B	
C 55	The first Model C	(See Appendix C)

> 5 Model A's
> 29 Model B's

The B prefixes above are to differentiate models only
All Model B's had an A prefix similar to the Model A's

Appendix C

PRODUCTION DATA PERTAINING TO MODELS C, E, AND F

—Author's notes—

The following three pages are scanned from Mr. Duane L. Bohnstedt's copy of pages of James Ward Packard's personal notebook pertaining to the production of Models C, E and the first Fs in Warren. Mr. Bohnstedt was an employee of the Packard Motor Car Company in 1956. He not only had great interest in the company history, but also had access to the company files during the final years in Detroit. Knowing of my interest in the Packard story, he shared these papers with me in 1973.

Comments:

1. Using Mr. Bohnstedt's numbers I have come to the conclusion 82 C's were built. Possibly he subtracted the number of the first 'C' (55) from the number of the last 'C' (140) to calculate his result. If so he did not count the first 'C' – a common mistake! The correct number of 'C's is obtained by subtracting the number of the last 'B' (54) from the number of the last 'C' (140). This number less the Model E and the first three 'F's (4 vehicles) results in a total of eighty-two Model Cs produced. (140 – 54 = 86 minus 4 being 82).

2. Unit 71, the one and only Model E was completed September 16, 1901, according to W.D. Packard's diary. It became the predecessor of the Model F. (See page 73).

3. Unit 121, the second F, along with F-100, was shipped to New York on October 30th, 1901, for the 2nd National Auto Show – W.D. Packard's diary.

4. Photos indicate that the first Fs sent to the Show were built on a Model C chassis. These vehicles were most likely updated before they were given production numbers and sold.

5. The first two Model C Specials (the prototypes), Ward Packard and George Weiss had built for themselves, had no recorded identification numbers. They started work on these vehicles in March, 1900, when the As and Bs were the focal point of their production effort. (See page 59) It

is reasonable to believe the original Model C Specials, like the 1899 Model A, were never assigned production numbers.

6. I have no idea how Mr. Bohnstedt arrived at the number of 50 Bs but the unit numbers do not support this many.

Appendix C

Duane L. Bohnstedt
11088 Timberline Drive
Utica, Michigan 48087

IDENTIFICATION LIST OF "PACKARD AUTOMOBILES" BUILT IN WARREN, OHIO.

This list was copied from a personal notebook of James Ward Packard in Sept. 1956. It is copied from the original with 'crossouts', changes etc. as they appeared.

C-55 First 'C' made.
C-56 First production 'C'. Sold to Charles C. Otis, Yonkers, N.Y. Tonneau Body, Had 12 tooth sprocket-20 M.P.H. speed.
C-57 H.S. Woodsworth, Rochester, N.Y. First 12 had same machinery. Same as C-56 except body.
C-58 Hugh S. Rose, Geneva, N.Y. Standard Carriage, same as C-56.
C-59 Adams & McMurtry. Same as C-56.
C-60 Adams & McMurtry. Same as C-56.
C-61 George D. Adams, Cleveland, Ohio. Same as C-56.
C-62 Mr. Evans, Buffalo, N.Y. Same as C-56.
C-63 Adams & McMurtry
C-64 George E. Warner, Buffalo, N.Y. Yellow body, wooden wheels. Same as C-56.
C-65 Mr. Clarence Havland, Akron, Ohio. Same as C-56 except for wooden wheels.
C-66 Wm. Rockefeller, Yonkers, N.Y. Top, seat straps. Same as C-56.
C-67 H.B. Shattuck & Son. Boston. Same as C-56.
C-68 Spl. Dr. Martin, Buffalo, N.Y. White body, wooden wheels.
C-69 Spl. J.S. Breez Breese, N.Y. Red body, wire wheels.
C-70 Spl. McMurtry, N.Y. Black body.

E-71 J.W. Packard, Warren, Ohio. A special carriage all around. Practically all parts different.

C-72 (Starts Lot 13) John M. Satterfield, Buffalo, N.Y. Blue body, Red running gear. First lot of 13 carriages. These carriages have stiff steering post & new worm gear casing, also new cast iron exhaust valve casting and head (looks like bearing) cylinder plugged for magneto.
C-73 George G. McMurtry, N.Y. Same as C-72. Had canopy top & tonneau.
C-74 Adams & McMurtry, N.Y.
C-75 B.F. Harris Jr. Champaigne, Ill. Standard C tonneau.
C-76 Joseph T. Speer, Pittsburg, Pa. % Adams & McMurtry. Same as C-72.
C-77 Adams & McMurtry. Same as C-72.
C-78 J.W. Lee Jr., Cleveland, Ohio. Standard C carriage. Same as C-72.
C-79 Miss Fletcher, (Detroit), % Adams & McMurtry. Same as C-72.
C-80 H.B. Shattuck & Son. Same as C-72.

C-81 George T. Steadman, St Louis, Mo. Same as C-72.
C-82 H. J. Coleman, La Cross, Wisc. Same as C-72.
C-83 Dr. E. M. Seuseuey, St Louis, Mo. Same as C-72.
C-84 Adams & McMurtry, N.Y. Last of "Lot 13" Same as C-72.

C-85 Dr. Hugo A. Auler 814 S. 8th. St. St Louis, Mo.
      First lot of 25 Cs. One lot of 12 & one lot of 13 Cs previous to this lot.
      Practically no change in the construction. (connection of governor shaft change)
C-86
C-87
C-88 Adams & McMurtry. Same as C-85. First lot of 25 Cs.
C-89
C-90 H. B. Shattuck
C-91 J. E. Easton, LaCross, Wisc. Same as C-85.
C-92 H. B. Shattuck & Son. Same as C-85.
C-93 Adams & McMurtry. Same as C-85.
C-94 H. B. Shattuck & Son. Same as C-85.
C-95
C-96 W.F. Butts. Buffalo, N.Y. (This name crossed out and Spencer Kelly added)
      Same as C-85.
C-97
C-98
C-99

F-100 First 'F' Carriage at factory, December/January 1st. 1903 (This date may be
      in error--D.L.B. August 1973)

C-101 Henry Chisholm, Cleveland, Ohio.
C-102 Henry Todd, Youngstown, Ohio.
C-103 Henry Stanbaugh (may be Stawbaugh), Youngstown, Ohio.
C-104
C-105 Victor B. Buck, Los Angeles, California.
C-106 R. H. Tifft, Buffalo, N.Y.
C-107 A. B. Wright, Buffalo, N.Y.
C-108 Mr. Shrigley, Boston, Mass. % Shattuck & Son. Same as C-85.
C-109

C-110 First of second lot of 25 Cs.
C-111
C-112 L. S. Ovitt, Waukesha, Wisc.
C-113
C-114
C-115
C-116 Henry Clapp, Attleboro, Mass.
C-117
C-118
C-119
C-120

Appendix C

F-121   Second 'F' made.

C-122
C-123
C-124   Louis Perriu, Trenton, N.J.
C-125
C-126
C-127   E.H. Bennett, Elizabeth, N.Y. (a penciled in notation says that this was the 3rd.'F').
C-128
C-129   C.E. Burke, Cleveland, Ohio.
C-130   George W. Welles, Southbridge, Mass.
C-131   Andrew F. West, Buffalo, N.Y.
C-132
C-133   R.M. Randall, Saginaw, Mich.
C-134
C-135
C-136
C-137   J.Q. Adams, Eureka, S.D.
C-138   N. Libert, St Cloud, Minn.
C-139   Pardee & Co.
C-140   Pardee & Co. This was the last of the "C"s.

From what I have been able to determine there were 5 'A' models built, 50 'B's and 81 'C's. It appears that 'B' models carried numbers with an "A" prefix with "C" used for "C" models.

There was no 'C'-71--71 was designated an 'E' and was a special vehicle built for J.W. Packard.
The number 100 was assigned to the first 'F' model. 121 to the second.
C-127 was designated as a 'C', but according to J.W.s notes it was really the third 'F'.

Duane L. Bohnstedt
Utica, Michigan
August 23, 1973

Appendix D

The following letter to George L. Weiss from James Ward Packard, dated May 9, 1900, gives a clue as to the number of units produced before the Model Cs went into production.

The Mr. Harris mentioned in the letter had to have been Al. F. Harris whose brothers received Model As on May 7th and May 17th. Mr. Packard states Harris had one on order but he had not heard from him. Therefore, he decided to send the Harris car to Mr. August Veghte of Troy, N.Y. who had ordered a car from Mr. Weiss before this letter was written. He must have been anxious to receive it. This vehicle was, without much doubt, the first production Model B.

Also in this letter Mr. Packard writes: "within two weeks [he] will be ready to order material for 24 more carriages". When these 24 carriages are added to the production figures, verified in the Packard & Weiss ledger (see Appendix B), the total of 29 'B's can be confirmed. B-31 through B-54 being 24.

Unfortunately the orders for these 24 units do not appear in the partnership ledger. Another set of books must have been opened but there is no record of them. The partners were already considering incorporation by July 1900.

It is interesting to note this letter was signed by Mr. Packard's secretary. The stamp in the lower right hand margin reads:

"Mr. J.W. Packard was obliged to leave this office
before the foregoing, personally dictated letter
could be made ready for his signature."

Appendix D

My dear George:-

We have just received the lighter pair of springs for fly wheels of your carriage and I have sent them to Ions requesting him to put them in. I have also written Mrs. Weiss telling her that Ions will call for the carriage. I realize that you may possible be perfectly contented with the set in there, but I consider it necessary that we try this experiment so that we can finally determine on the exact stiffness of springs necessary to use. I trust that my action in this matter meets with your approval.

I expect to go east today and will probably be back the first part of next week. I had counted on exercising your carriage somewhat this week, but will have to put it off until later. We are getting along very well in the shop now and within two weeks will be ready to order material for 24 more carriages. I have not heard from the Mr. Harris to whom this last carriage was sold, but am fitting it up to go to Troy and think that we can ship it the last of next week. I will advise you just as soon as I hear from him.

Mr. Geo. L. Weiss,
  Southern Hotel, St. Louis

Yours very truly,
J. W. Packard
msa

Letter from James Ward Packard to George L. Weiss concerning Model B production.

Appendix E

APPENDIX E
WARREN, OHIO, BUILT CARS KNOWN TO EXIST

#	YEAR	MODEL	ENGINE NO.	BODY STYLE	CURRENT OWNER	YEAR ACQUIRED	CITY & STATE	ORIGINAL OWNER STATE & CITY
1	1899	A	None	4 Pass Carriage w/dos-a-dos rear seat	Lehigh University	-1930-	Bethlehem, PA	Factory - never sold
2	1900	B	A30	4 Pass Carriage w/dos-a-dos rear seat	Terry Martin	-1972-	Warren, OH	George Blackmore, Painsville, OH
3	1900	B	A39	4 Pass Carriage w/dos-a-dos rear seat	National Auto Museum	-1959-	Reno, NV	Unknown
4	1901	C	C67	4 Pass Carriage w/dos-a-dos rear seat	Carl Schmitt	-1990-	Walla Walla, WA	H.B. Shattuck & Son, Boston, MA
5	1901	C	C96	4 Pass Carriage w/dos-a-dos rear seat	Crawford Museum	-1972-	Cleveland, OH	Spencer Kelly, Buffalo, NY
6	1901	C	C103	4 Pass Carriage w/dos-a-dos rear seat	John Hovey	-1986-	Wyckoff, NJ	Henry Stambaugh, Youngstown, OH
7	1901	C	C105	4 Pass Carriage w/dos-a-dos rear seat	Studebaker Museum	-1958-	South Bend, IN	Victor B. Buck, Los Angeles, CA
8	1901	C	C117	Six Pass Rear Entrance Tonneau	Bob McKeown	-2003-	Perryopolis, PA	H.B. Shattuck & Son, Boston, MA
9	1902	F	F163	4 Pass Detachable Tonneau	Jim Brodes	-1984-	Tucson, AZ	NY?
10	1902	F	F165	4 Pass Detachable Tonneau	Nancy Matthews	-1986-	Woodside, CA	A. J. Wheatherhead, Cleveland, OH?
11	1902	F	F201	4 Pass Detachable Tonneau	Howard Schaevitz	-1996-	Edgewater Park, NJ	R. E. Bousfield, Bay City, MI
12	1902	F	F233	4 Pass Detachable Tonneau	Bob McKeown	-2001-	Perryopolis, PA	CA?
13	1902	G	G242	5 Pass Detachable Tonneau	Ann Bothwell	-1937-	Woodland Hills, CA	Factory Callback?
14	1903	F	F251	5 Pass Detachable Tonneau	Drew Lewis	-1998-	Lederach, PA	Packard Montreal, Quebec
15	1903	F	F322	2 Pass Roadster- "Old Pacific"	Ford Museum	-1933-	Dearborn, MI	Factory - never sold
16	1903	F	F355	5 Pass Detachable Tonneau	Bob McKeown	-2003-	Perryopolis, PA	Colorado
17	1903	F	F356	5 Pass Detachable Tonneau	Terry Martin	-1986-	Warren, OH	WI
18	1903	F	F387	2 Pass Roadster ("Old Pacific II")	Nat. Packard Museum	-1999-	Warren, OH	Unknown
19	1903	K	K401	Gray Wolf	Citizens Motorcar Co.	?	Dayton, OH	Race Car

INDEX

Adams, George B.
  McMurtry joins as partner, 71
  New York Sales Office opens, 71
Adams-McMurtry Co, formed, 71
  advertisements, 83, 127
  company purchased by Packard Motor Car Co., 125
  description of new facilities, 93
  Joy and Newberry visit, 97
  move to 59th St., 91
Adjutant Quartermaster General,
  Col. Jacob Weiss, 27
ALAM, Association of Licensed Automobile Manufacturers, 125
Alden, PA, 28
Alger, Russell A., 114
  elected director, 129
  sent to Warren to deter James Ward Packard resigning, 137
  voted Vice President, 145
American Railroad Signal Co., 159
American Union Telegraph Co., 17
Anthracite Coal, 28
"Ask the Man Who Owns One", first used in advertisement, 83
Atlantic & Great Western Railroad, 15
Automatic Spark Advance, 53
Automobile Club of America, 65
  Albert Shattuck, president, 71 sponsored:
    National Auto Shows, 69, 89, 129
    New York to Buffalo run, 77
    New York to Boston Time Trial, 111, 113
Automobile Magazine, The
  Adams-McMurtry's new facilities, 91, 93
  Krarup, Marius C., Editor, joins Fetch on transcontinental run, 141
Automobile and Motor Review, The
  Criticizes Model G, 107, 111
Automobile Quarterly, 9

Baker Electric, 97
Balfour, A. J., 11
Barnum, Rolla, 15
Berry, Nancy Ann, 13
Beverly Hills, CA, 10, 159
Bishop, David Wolfe, 79
Blackmore, George,
  buys Model B (A-30), 49
  first dealership, 127
  placed ads in *Horseless Age*, 127
Blousfield, C. J., (Bay City, MI, dealer), 127
"Blue Devil", Joy's Model F, 101, 111
Boyer, Joseph, 129
Brady, Diamond Jim, 29
Brown, George, Winton General Manager, 31

Brooks, James, 15
Bruder, Kathryn, 155, 157
Burlington and Quincy Railroad, 95
Butler Drawbar Attachment Co., 27, 159

Camp, Alanson, 15
Camp, Sylvia, 15
Carbon County, PA, 29
Case School, Cleveland, OH, 59
Chaffee, Charles Cook, company chauffeur, 77
Chicago Times Herald, 23
Chronicle, Warren, 47, 147
Cist, Jacob, 28
Civil War, 15
Clapp, H. E., Mt. Washington in Model C, 107
Cleveland Forge & Iron, 27
Cleveland Plain Dealer,
  names the Gray Wolf, 143, 145
Cook, Madison, 15
Costain, A.B., (San Francisco dealer), 127
Cowles, Edward P., 23, 25
Cox, Rebecca, 27
Cripper & Church, (Los Angeles dealer), 127
Crocker, Sewall K., Dr. Nelson's mechanic – Winton transcontinental trip, 139
Dealerships, 127
DeDion-Bouton, 23, 25, 27
Detroit Free Press, covers Joy's Packard auto, stock purchases, 97
  sale of Packard Motor Car Co. 97, 99
Delphi Corp, 21, 156
Dingle, Edith Weiss, 9
"Dispense with the Horse", 21
Doud, Mary Elizabeth, 17, 155
Doud, William Chapman, 17

Eckley, PA, 28
Electric Vehicle Co., 125
Evans, Ellicott, (Buffalo dealer), 77

Ford, Henry, 89, 125
Forged iron products, 15
Fetch, Tom
  transcontinental trip, 141
Founders of the ALAM, 125
Franklin, Benjamin, 27

General Electric, 155
General Motors Corp., 21, 156
Gilmer, Elizabeth A., 151
Graham, Milton, 9
Greene, General Nathanael, 27
Gray Wolf – Model K race car, named by *Cleveland Plain Dealer*, 143, 145

H gearshift pattern, 45
Hackett, Walter, W.D Packard's secretary, 109
   addresses quality of materials, 109
Harris, Charles G.
   buys fourth production car, 47
   involved in first local auto accident with John McNutt, 57
Harris, Fred W.
   buys fifth production car, 47
Hatcher, William Albert (Bert), 33
   designs all single cylinder engines, 59
   joins the company, 41
   placed in charge of drafting room, 41
   receives 55 shares of Ohio Automobile Co. stock, 75
   resigns from Packard Motor Car Co., 127
   starts his own company, 129
Honeywell, Hollis, 69
Horseless Age, The, 23, 43, 49
   Chicago to New York City trip – E.B. Martin, 107
   criticizes Model G, 113
   describes Model E, 73
   reports H.B. Wick's offer to buy half interest in Ohio Automobile Co., 115
Howry, W. D., 25
Huff, Russell, mechanical engineer
   asst. engineer under Schmidt, 147
   chief engineer 1905, 147
   hired, 59
   heads Experimental Department, 147

Ions, W.S.
   drives K No. 1 Warren to Detroit, 135

Jackson, Dr. Horatio Nelson, makes first transcontinental trip in Winton, 139
Joy, Henry Bourne, 10, 95, 149
   ALAM meeting in New York City with J.W.Packard re Selden Patent, 125
   begins to influence company's affairs, 101
   buys Baker Electric for wife, 97
   buys first company shares, Nov. 1901, 97
   buys 150 additional shares, attends stockholders' meeting, 97
   buys one-year old Packard, orders Model F, 97
   chooses Albert Kahn as architect for Detroit plant, 123
   early business experience, 95
   education, 95
   enters New York to Boston time trial with "Blue Devil", 111
   praises Packard auto to press, 97
   receives Model F, named "Blue Devil", 101
   sets Detroit move deadline, 125
   solicits J.W.Packard's input for new Detroit plant, 121
   visits Adams-McMurtry, 97

Kahn, Albert
   American Architecture Magazine Scholarship award, 123
   architect chosen to design new plant, 123
   establishes industrial plant guidelines for future auto plants, 123
   Packard Motor Car Co. commission was first large project, 123
Kimes, Beverly Rae, 9, 11
Kreiger, Adolph O., representative of Daimler Works, 63
Kirkham, George D.
   buys first Packard sold to party outside of the company, 47
Krarup, Marius C.
   editor of *The Automobile* magazine, 141
   joins Tom Fetch in transcontinental run, 141
   takes photos and publicizes trip, 141

Lake Chautauqua, NY, 15, 23
Lakewood, NY, 15
Leach, Benjamin, 13
Leach, Julia Ann 13
Lehigh Canal, 28
Lehigh Coal Mine Co. 28
Lehighton, PA, 28
Lehigh University, 19, 151, 153
Lehigh Water Gap, 27, 28
Long Beach, CA, 159
Long Island Auto Club, 107
   sponsors Jamaica – Oyster Bay and return contest, 107

Machinist strike, 89
Madison Square Garden, 69
Mansfield Normal School, 28
Mansfield, PA, 28
March, Fred C.
   drives a Model F in New York to Boston Time Trial, 111
   represents Company in Jamaica to Oyster Bay contest, 107
   Martin, E.B., drives his Model F from Chicago to New York City, 107
Martin, Terry, 9, 11, 12
McCarty, Walter, (Beverly Hills developer), 159
McMillan, Phillip, Board of Directors, 129
McMurtry, Alden L.
   declines purchase of Model E, 47
   joins George Adams as partner in New York office, 71, 77
   represents Company in Jamaica – Oyster Bay run, 107
McNutt, John F., early Model B owner
   involved in first local auto accident, 57
Metzger & Co. (Detroit dealer), 127
Michigan Central, Burlington and Quincy Railroads, 95
Model A, 43, 45, 47, 91, 99

Index

Model B 49, 53, 69, 91, 99
Model C, 59, 69, 91, 99, 107
Model E, 73, 91
Model F, 89, 91, 99, 101, 131
Model G, 105, 107
Model K
   introduced at New York Auto Show, 129
   Model K developed into race car as the Gray Wolf, 143
   Packard Motor Car Co. buys back and scraps 25 Ks, 145
   problems persist 129, 131
   problems cause friction between Joy and James Ward Packard, 135
   W.S. Ions drives first K from Warren to Detroit, 135
Model L
   defects in K corrected in Model L, designed in Warren, 145
   first model produced in Detroit, 145
Model M
   complicated coring causes problems, 131, 133
   conceived as single cylinder competitor for curved dash Oldsmobile, 131
   development shelved in favor of L, 145
   emerged as two cylinder vehicle, 133
   James Ward Packard labels it "not very promising", 133
   M project discontinued, 139
Molly McGuires, 29
Moore, C.J.
   becomes plant manager in Detroit, 147
   hired to help Schmidt with K problems, 113
Moravian Church, 28
Motor Age, 83
Motor magazine
   Walter Hackett article describes early problems with quality of materials, 109
Motor Vehicle Review, 49
   describes new Model Cs, 59

Naphtha launch, Lake Chautauqua, 23, 25
National Automobile Shows – Madison Square Garden, New York City isponsored by Auto Club of America
   First – November 1900, Model B and C displayed, 69
   Second – November 1901, Model C and F displayed, optimum number of cylinders discussed, 89
   Third – Jan. 1903. Sidney Waldon assumes duties of George Weiss, 125
   Model K introduced, 129
National Electric Lamp Assoc. (NELA), 155
National Packard Museum, 10
National Railroad Convention, Saratoga Springs, NY
   Weiss and Winton take their autos, 31

Nelson, A.C., early draftsman, 41
Newberry, Truman H.–Joy's brother-in-law, 95
   blames James Ward Packard for K problems and causes James Ward Packard to consider resignation, 137
   drives K to Watch Hill, - has problems, 137
   elected Director PMCC, 129
   owns Model F named the "Red Devil", 101
   reprimanded by Joy, 137
   visit to Adams-McMurtry with Joy, 97
New York to Boston Time Trial
   sponsored by Auto Club of America
   Weiss and Harlan W. Whipple awarded medals – top honors, 113
   contestants listed, 111
New York to Buffalo Endurance Run, 77, 79, 81, 83
   Albert R. Shattuck, Boston Packard dealer, entered a French Panhard, 79
   five Packards entered, 77
   list of drivers, 77
   Packards receive top American honors, 83
   run cut short due to death of President McKinley, 81
New York and Ohio Co., 21, 23, 25, 41, 63, 75, 151, 156

Ohio Automobile Co., 11, 65
   Adams-McMurtry partnership formed, 71
   became New York State dealers, 71
   additional land purchased, 75
   buildings and machinery purchased, 75
   capitalization reduced, 75
   Charles Schmidt hired, 101
   decision to elect new directors, 113
   distribution of responsibilities, 63
   eastern sales office opened in New York City, 71
   exhibits at first National Auto Show, 69
   first ads in *Horseless Age*, 65, 127
   $40,000 of orders on hand, Jan. 1901, 71
   fourth factory building started, 107
   H.B. Shattuck named northeast sales representative, 71
   increase in capital stock approved to accommodate Detroit investors, 113
   increase in size and price of Packards, 99
   last stockholders' meeting where founders would be in control, 113
   Long Island Auto Club – Jamaica – Oyster Bay run. Fred March and Alden McMurtry represent Company, 107
   machinists' strike, 89
   Model E built, 73
   Model F selling well, 107, 110
   new 12,000 sq. ft. building completed, 99
   New York to Buffalo Endurance Run, 77, 79, 81, 83

officers elected, 65
optimum number of cylinders debate, 103
outside capital needed, 77
poor materials cause problems, 109
2nd New York Auto Show and Model F, 89
special stockholders' meeting Oct 1902, 109
stock distribution, to partners and Hatcher, 75
Old Pacific, name given to Model F on transcontinental run, 141
Ohio State University, 17
Otis, Charles C., 71

Packard, A History of the Motor Car and The Company, 9, 11
Packard, Alaska, 17
Packard, Andrew J., 15
Packard, B.F., 15
Packard, Carlotta, 17
Packard, Cornelia Olive, 17
Packard, Daniel Berry, 15
Packard Electric Co., 19, 21, 151, 155, 156
Packard, Harry, 15, 17
Packard, James Ward
   additional capital required, 59, 63, 114
   agrees to stay until move to Detroit is completed, 137
   Alexander Winton rebuffs suggested changes to Winton, 37
   ALAM meeting, attends with Joy, 125
   automobiles in estate, 154
   blamed for defects in Model K by Newberry, 137
   business activities after 1903:
     New York & Ohio Co., 151
     Packard Electric, 19, 21, 151, 155
       initiates harness production, 151 Wolcott, Newton, takes over, 156
   Cleveland to Buffalo run with Weiss, 57
   diary entry "Joy takes full charge", 145
   Detroit plant planning, involvement, 123
   early years, 19
   final days, (cancer), 153
   graduates from Lehigh University, 19
   Hatcher hired, 41
   hobbies:
     clocks and watches collection, 152
     firearms collection, 152
   "Honorary Presidency", relinquishes, 152
   has no control over work in Warren, 137
   Joy apologizes for Newberry, 137
   Joy, has argument with, 129, 131
   Joy visits Detroit with, 114
   marries Elizabeth Gilmer, 151
   meets George L. Weiss, 33
   Model E, purchases, 73
   Model M, "not promising",, 133
   Mother dies – returns to Warren, 149
   move to Detroit, denies, 117

Number One Packard completed, 43
Number One Packard transmission modified, 45
Ohio Automobile Co., elected President, 65
Packard Electric Co., cofounder of, 19
Park Avenue home, purchases, (now Buckeye Club), 152
partners invest $3000 each, 39
philanthropic gifts, 153, 154
potential investors, meets with, 114
requests architect to be sent to Warren, 121
resignation, tenders, 137
retirement, 151
Sawyer Man Electric Co., New York, employed by, 19
shares awarded in lieu of salary, 75
single cylinder engine, prefers, 89, 103
unhappy with Warren situation, 139
Ward & Hatcher share design work, 43
Weiss, offers partnership to, 37, 39
Weiss resignation, opposes, 119
Winton #13, purchase, 27, 33
Winton #13, troubles with, 33, 35
Winton factory, makes last trip to, 37
writes Weiss re 24 more Model Bs, 47
Packard, John, 15
Packard Historical Handbook #3, 137
Packard Magazine, 121
Packard, Mary E. Doud, 17, 155
Packard Motor Car Company
   Adams-McMurtry, purchased by, 125
   Detroit directors elected, 129
   Detroit factory plans completed, 135
   Detroit investors take control, 115, 117
   election of new officers, 145
   four cylinder K shows speed capability, 143
   Gray Wolf – Schmidt's project, 143
   Hatcher resigns, 127
   Huff starts Experimental Dept., 147
   James Ward Packard named "Honorary President", 145
   Ward Packard threatens to resign, 137
   Joy – James Ward Packard rift, 135
   Joy takes over management, 145, 151
   Joy wants car like the Oldsmobile, 131
   land purchased for Detroit plant, 135
   last Warren building completed, 139
   Models F, G, K, L & M, designed, built, tested during 1903, 139
   Model F, a financial success, 139
   Model F production numbers, 139
   Model K defects corrected in Model L, 145
   Model K introduced, 129
   Model K is a failure, 145
   Model K problems, 135
   Model Ks recalled, 145
   Model M casting problems, 133
   Model M described, 131

Index

Model M designed, 131
Model M plans shelved, 133
move to Detroit begins, 147
multi cylinder design emphasis, 127
Old Pacific crosses country with Fetch and Krarup, 139, 141
Packard name adopted, 113
Schmidt takes over Hatcher's duties, 127
Waldon assumes Weiss' duties, 121
Waldon hired, 121
Warren employees, many move to Detroit, 147
Warren plant closes, 147, 149
Weiss resigns, 117, 119
workload overwhelming in Warren, 139
Packard Pointers, 121
Packard, Rolla, 12
Packard, Samuel, 12
Packard, Thomas, 12
Packard, Warren, 15, 17
Packard, Warren II, 25, 155
Packard & Weiss Partnership
  decision to build more automobiles, 45
  design flaws corrected, 57
  expenses exceeding income, 59
  fabrication & purchase of parts begins, 43
  first engine completed and tested, 43
  first vehicles go to partners, 47
  founders invest $3000 each, 39
  Hatcher hired, 41
  Huff, Russell hired, 59
  incorporation discussed, 63
  investors, search for new, 59, 63
  Model A first sales (in house), 47
  Model A first sale to outside party, 47
  Model B design completed, 47
  Model Cs – two prototypes built, 59
  Ohio Automobile Co. formed, 65
  partnership formalized, 45
  patents applied for, 49, 53
  publicity run Cleveland to Buffalo, 57
  Packard # 1 road tested, 43
  Ward and Hatcher design first carriage, 41
  Ward Packard & G.L. Weiss meet, 31
  Ward Packard buys Winton # 13, 33
  Weiss becomes partner, 35, 37, 39
  W.D. Packard opens ledger, 41
  work done in New York & Ohio Co. shops, 41
Packard, William C., 12
Packard, William Doud, 31
  Annie Packard dies, 155
  bank loan considered, 115
  business activities after 1903, 156
  builds homes in Warren and Chautauqua, 156
  buys second Packard built, 47
  early years, 17
  elected Secretary/Treasurer Ohio Automobile Co., 65
  employment, 17, 19, 21
  final days, 156, 157
  investigates autos in Europe, 39
  involved in other family businesses, 77
  joins Ward, forms Packard Electric Co., 21
  joins Ward in auto partnership, 41
  marries Annie Hadly Storer, 155
  opens Packard & Weiss Ledger, 41
  philanthropic gifts, 156, 157
  receives 100 share distribution, 75
  remarries, Kathryn Bruder, 155, 157
  struggles with financing, 115
  wants to sell auto business, 115
  Warren Packard II born, 155
Pardee Co., (Chicago dealer), 127
Patents:
  applied for, 49, 53
  in the name of Packard & Weiss, 41
Panhard, 79, 83
Patek, Philippe & Co., 152
Peale, John W., 21, 63

Quartermaster General, Adjutant, 27

Railroads, 15, 95
Revolutionary War, 27
Rockefeller, William, 104, 107, 134
Rockefeller, William D., 69

Satterfield, John M., 77, 83
Sawyer-Man Electric Co., 19
Schmidt, Charles
  designs Gray Wolf based on Model K engine, 143
  designs the Model K, 125
  engine designer for Mors Co., 103
  given full charge of production plus some design, 103
  hired at Joy's suggestion, 101
  influences multi-cylinder designs, 103, 105, 114
  involved with Model M design, 133
  problems with K, 131, 135
  takes over Hatcher's duties, 125
  takes job at Peerless Motor Car Co., 147
Schryver, Henry A., 25
Selden, George B., 125
Selden patent, 125
Shanks, Charles, Winton publicist, 31
Shattuck, Albert R., President, Auto Club of America, 71
  assigned Northeast territory, 71
Shattuck, H.B. & Son, 71
  Boston auto dealer – all makes, 71
  enters Panhard in New York to Buffalo Endurance Trial, 79
Smith, Ben, driver for H.B. Shattuck & Son, 79
Spark advance, automatic, 53
Stockholders Meetings
  October 24, 1900, 65

181

April 30, 1901 – election of officers, 71
January 29, 1902 – Joy attends for first time, 97
October 19, 1902 – name change, 113,114
January 29, 1903 – new board of directors,
   7(founders lose control), 113
February 5, 1903 – first board meeting in
   Detroit, (M approved), 131
May 19, 1903 – Detroit land purchase, 135
September 8, 1903 – new officers elected, 145
Strike, machinist, 89
Strong Talk, first Packard newsletter, 121
Studebaker Museum, 11

Teakle and Golden – awarded construction
   contract, 135
Turreff, Laura Lydia, 29
Turreff, William Fleming, 29

Veghte, August – buys first Model B, 49

Waldheim, Germany, 27
Waldon, Sidney
   assumes duties of Weiss, 121
   hired as advertising manager, 121
   originates *Packard Pointers*, 121
   originates *Strong Talk* 1st newsletter,121
   reports recall of all Model Ks, 145
   transcontinental trip, 139
   wants Joy to take over reins, 143
Warren Chronicle,(reports move), 47, 147
Warren power generating plant, 19
Warren Tribune (Ward denies move), 21, 117
Watch Hill, RI, 135, 137, 143
Weiss, Charles H., 28
   carriage business in Lehighton, PA,, 29
   patent for brake improvement, 29
Weiss, Francis, 28
Weiss, George Lewis
   approves hiring of Schmidt, 103
   arranges Adams-McMurtry formation, 71
   assigns H.B. Shattuck NE territory, 71
   assists Joy with car purchase, 97
   automotive affairs, remains active in, 159
   builds home in Beverly Hills, CA, 159
   business activities after resignation:
     American Railroad Signal Co. 159
     Butler Drawbar & Attachment Co., 159
   buys 3rd Packard built, 47
   buys Winton # 4, 31
   defends Model G, 111
   drives in New York to Boston run, 113
   drives with Ward in New York to Buffalo
     endurance run, 77, 79, 81, 83
   early years, Eckley, PA, 28
   education, 28
   elected vice president Ohio Automobile
     company, 65
   enters into partnership with Packard brothers,
     37, 39

   final years, 159, 160
   invests in Winton stock, 31
   invests $3000 with Packard brothers,39, 41
   invests with Walter McCarty, 159
   joins father-in-law's business, 29
   joins Ward in Cleveland-Buffalo publicity run,
     57
   manages marketing, 77
   marries Laura Lydia Turreff, 29
   meets Packard brothers, 33
   moves to Cleveland, Ohio, 29
   moves to Southern California, 159
   Ohio Automobile Co., helped form, 65
   organizes Packard exhibit at first National Auto
     Show, 69
   press contacts, handles, 69
   receives stock in lieu of salary, 75
   resents Detroit investors takeover, 114
   resigns from Packard Motor Car Co., 114
   retirement, 159
   sees Packard # 1 completed, 43
   sells Packards in Cleveland, OH, 55
   sells Winton stock, 39
   sets up dealerships, 69
   trades Packard stock for automobiles, 119, 159
Weiss, Col. Jacob, 27, 28
Weiss, Dr. Johann, 27
Weissport, PA,, 28
Westinghouse, 19
Westinghouse Air Brake, 27
White, Roger Turreff, 12
Wick, H.B.
   offers to buy half interest in company, 115
Whipple, Harlan W.
   enters Model G in New York to Boston Time
     Trial, 111, 113
Winton, Alexander, 27, 29, 31, 33, 35, 37
Winton Motor Carriage Co., 10, 11, 27, 29, 31,
   33, 37
Winslow, Randolph, (Philadelphia dealer), 127
Wisell, Eli K., 15
Wolcott, Newton A., 151, 156